TUNG JEN'S

CHINESE ASTROLOGY

foulsham

London · New York · Toronto · Sydney

foulsham
Bennetts Close, Cippenham, Berks. SL1 5AP

DEDICATION
To Mi Di Su, without whom the trip
around the Chinese Zoo would not
have been half so much fun.

ISBN 0–572–01893–2

Printed and bound in Great Britain by Cox & Wyman Ltd, Reading, Berkshire

CONTENTS

Chinese Animal Year List

OPERATIVE DATES	ELEMENT	SIGN
January 30, 1911, to February 17, 1912:	Metal	Pig
February 18, 1912, to February 5, 1913:	Water	Rat
February 6, 1913, to January 25, 1914:	Water	Ox
January 26, 1914, to February 13, 1915:	Wood	Tiger
February 14, 1915, to February 2, 1916:	Wood	Rabbit
February 3, 1916, to January 22, 1917:	Fire	Dragon
January 23, 1917, to February 10, 1918:	Fire	Snake
February 11, 1918, to January 31, 1919:	Earth	Horse
February 1, 1919, to February 18, 1920:	Earth	Goat
February 19, 1920, to February 7, 1921:	Metal	Monkey
February 8, 1921, to January 27, 1922:	Metal	Rooster
January 28, 1922, to February 15, 1923:	Water	Dog
February 16, 1923, to February 4, 1924:	Water	Pig
February 5, 1924, to January 23, 1925:	Wood	Rat
January 24, 1925, to February 11, 1926:	Wood	Ox
February 12, 1926, to February 1, 1927:	Fire	Tiger
February 2, 1927, to January 21, 1928:	Fire	Rabbit
January 22, 1928, to February 8, 1929:	Earth	Dragon
February 9, 1929, to January 28, 1930:	Earth	Snake
January 29, 1930, to February 16, 1931:	Metal	Horse
February 17, 1931, to February 5, 1932:	Metal	Goat
February 6, 1932, to January 24, 1933:	Water	Monkey
January 25, 1933, to February 13, 1934:	Water	Rooster
February 14, 1934, to February 2, 1935:	Wood	Dog
February 3, 1935, to January 23, 1936:	Wood	Pig
January 24, 1936, to February 10, 1937:	Fire	Rat
February 11, 1937, to January 30, 1938:	Fire	Ox
January 31, 1938, to February 18, 1939:	Earth	Tiger
February 19, 1939, to February 7, 1940:	Earth	Rabbit
February 8, 1940, to January 26, 1941:	Metal	Dragon
January 27, 1941, to February 14, 1942:	Metal	Snake
February 15, 1942, to February 3, 1943:	Water	Horse
February 4, 1943, to January 24, 1944:	Water	Goat
January 25, 1944, to February 11, 1945:	Wood	Monkey
February 12, 1945, to February 1, 1946:	Wood	Rooster
February 2, 1946, to January 21, 1947:	Fire	Dog
January 22, 1947, to February 9, 1948:	Fire	Pig
February 10, 1948, to January 28, 1949:	Earth	Rat
January 29, 1949, to February 15, 1950:	Earth	Ox
February 16, 1950, to February 5, 1951:	Metal	Tiger
February 6, 1951, to January 25, 1952:	Metal	Rabbit
January 26, 1952, to February 13, 1953:	Water	Dragon
February 14, 1953, to February 2, 1954:	Water	Snake
February 3, 1954, to January 23, 1955:	Wood	Horse

Chinese Animal Year List

OPERATIVE DATES	ELEMENT	SIGN
January 24, 1955, to February 10, 1956:	Wood	Goat
February 11, 1956, to January 29, 1957:	Fire	Monkey
January 30, 1957, to February 17, 1958:	Fire	Rooster
February 18, 1958, to February 6, 1959:	Earth	Dog
February 7, 1959, to January 27, 1960:	Earth	Pig
January 28, 1960, to February 14, 1961:	Metal	Rat
February 15, 1961, to February 4, 1962:	Metal	Ox
February 5, 1962, to January 24, 1963:	Water	Tiger
January 25, 1963, to February 12, 1964:	Water	Rabbit
February 13, 1964, to January 31, 1965:	Wood	Dragon
February 1, 1965, to January 20, 1966:	Wood	Snake
January 21, 1966, to February 8, 1967:	Fire	Horse
February 9, 1967, to January 28, 1968:	Fire	Goat
January 29, 1968, to February 15, 1969:	Earth	Monkey
February 16, 1969, to February 5, 1970:	Earth	Rooster
February 6, 1970, to January 25, 1971:	Metal	Dog
January 26, 1971, to February 14, 1972:	Metal	Pig
February 15, 1972, to February 2, 1973:	Water	Rat
February 3, 1973, to January 23, 1974:	Water	Ox
January 24, 1974, to February 10, 1975:	Wood	Tiger
February 11, 1975, to January 30, 1976:	Wood	Rabbit
January 31, 1976, to February 17, 1977:	Fire	Dragon
February 18, 1977, to February 6, 1978:	Fire	Snake
February 7, 1978, to January 27, 1979:	Earth	Horse
January 28, 1979, to February 15, 1980:	Earth	Goat
February 16, 1980, to February 4, 1981:	Metal	Monkey
February 5, 1981, to January 24, 1982:	Metal	Rooster
January 25, 1982, to February 12, 1983:	Water	Dog
February 13, 1983, to February 1. 1984:	Water	Pig
February 2, 1984, to February 19, 1985:	Wood	Rat
February 20, 1985, to February 8, 1986:	Wood	Ox
February 9, 1986, to January 28, 1987:	Fire	Tiger
January 29, 1987, to February 16, 1988:	Fire	Rabbit
February 17, 1988, to February 5, 1989:	Earth	Dragon
February 6, 1989, to January 25, 1990:	Earth	Snake
January 26, 1990, to February 13, 1991:	Metal	Horse
February 14, 1991, to February 2, 1992:	Metal	Goat
February 3, 1992, to January 21, 1993:	Water	Monkey
January 22, 1993, to February 9, 1994:	Water	Rooster
February 10, 1994, to January 30, 1995:	Wood	Dog
January 31, 1995, to February 18, 1996:	Wood	Pig
February 19, 1996, to February 6, 1997:	Fire	Rat
February 7, 1997, to January 27, 1998:	Fire	Ox
January 28, 1998, to February 15, 1999:	Earth	Tiger

ABOUT CHINESE ASTROLOGY

There is little doubt that Chinese astrologers were already looking at the stars and planets with interest when the first civilisations were starting to spring up in the Middle East, at least five thousand years ago. It may be partly as a result of the insular nature of the oriental peoples and their geographical remoteness that the observations of these wise old sages took them along slightly alternative paths to those adopted by Western astrologers, but whatever the reason, Chinese Astrology does differ somewhat to the more readily understood occidental form.

The Chinese were especially fascinated by the Moon, and although they clearly knew about the existence of all the major planets in the solar system, it was around the interactions of the Sun and Moon that at least the more popular branch of Chinese Astrology developed. The Chinese zodiac comprises twelve signs, exactly as in Western Astrology, though in the case of the oriental system, these are all given animal names. The actual origins of the animal signs are lost in the mists of time, though you will come to understand just how accurate many of them are when describing a personality type.

The Chinese set much store by the year in which a person was born, since each year was thought to be governed by a specific animal sign. Good or bad fortune for society as a whole was also tied to the animal in question and so an individual's approach to each year was very important. This is the part of Chinese astrology that the West has come to know, though as you will find out in the pages that follow, there is much more to Chinese astrology than this. Other aspects of singular importance when looking at what the Chinese have to say about you as an individual include your Chinese Moon Sign and the position of the 'Ascendant.'

Read on to gain a clearer understanding of what makes you the person that you are - courtesy of the deep understanding of human nature, inherent in one of the least understood and yet wisest cultures that the world has ever produced.

EXPLAINING CHINESE ASTROLOGY

To get the best out of this book it is important that you read this page and the following one very carefully. As with any branch of astrology, Eastern or Western, it is not one factor that goes to explain the type of nature that you have inherited from the day of your birth, but a number. This book allows you, step by step, to learn about your Chinese Year, the element that ruled that year, your Chinese Ascending Sign and also your Chinese Moon Sign. It is a combination of all these factors that ultimately sets the seal on your personality.

YOUR CHINESE ANIMAL YEAR

Finding out what animal sign ruled the year of your birth could not be easier. Just look for the Chinese year of your birth, on pages 4 and 5, making certain that you don't fall into a previous Chinese year if you were born in January or February. Alongside the year you will see the name of one of the Chinese animals. This is the sign that ruled the year of your birth.

Once you have established what your animal is, you can then turn straight away to the section between pages 9 and 80. In this section you will find an in-depth appraisal of all the animals in the oriental zoo. The good and bad points of the creature that rules your animal year will, to some extent, be mirrored in your own nature. However, since it is not possible for every person born in a twelve month period to have exactly the same personality, you should think of the Animal Year of your birth only as a starting point.

The Chinese were fascinated by the interaction of Sun, Moon and Planets, and by numbers. Although there are only twelve animal signs, each year governed by a sign is also subject to the influence of one of five Elements. The Elements obviously change at a different rate to the sign, so it is only possible for an animal sign and a specific Element to coincide once every 60 years. You may have noticed when you looked for the Chinese year of your birth, that in addition to your

Animal Sign, the name of an Element was also listed. You will find out more about your Element on page 81, and this is a further hint at refining the ultimate quality of your nature.

CHINESE RISING SIGNS

Each part of the day was ruled, the Chinese believed, by one of the twelve animal signs. It is fairly easy, as long as you know roughly what time of day you were born, to work out what sign ruled that hour. Instructions for this section of the book can be found on page 143. Taken together with your Animal Year Sign and Element, this will begin to form a more complex description of your own unique personality.

CHINESE MOON SIGNS

The Chinese observers of old maintained that each month of the year was ruled in its own right by a specific Animal Sign. Here we begin to recognise shades of traditional Western Astrology, because each Chinese Moon Sign relates pretty well to one of the Western Sun Signs. For example, the Chinese Moon of the Dragon is synonymous with the period known in the West as the Sign of Aries. Almost everyone knows what their Sun Sign is, and on page 184 you will find a list of these, together with their Chinese Moon counterparts. There are also interpretations so that you can see how your Chinese Moon Sign contributes to your overall nature.

AND FINALLY

Whether you are looking at your Element, Animal Year Sign, Rising Sign or Chinese Moon Sign, you can keep coming back to the original descriptions of the traditional Animal Signs, commencing on page 9, which are just as relevant, no matter what part of your astrological make-up you are looking at. With a combination of Element, Year, Ascendant and Moon, you could be an Earth Dragon - Horse - Pig for example, and each of these animals, together with their particular characteristics go towards making up the very special person that is you. Have fun, and marvel at the knowledge and foresight of those who made the fascinating connections on the rolling hills and vast plains of China all those years ago.

1900
1912
1924
1936
1948
1960
1972
1984
1996

ONE OWNER
£6999

The Rat

ABOUT THE RAT

It is an unfortunate fact that, in the West at least, the Rat has gained such an unfortunate reputation, for this animal is undoubtedly one of the cleverest and most resourceful creatures on the Earth. Staggering stories exist, bearing testimony to the tenacity, courage and downright cheek of this representative of the rodent family, which certainly had a bearing on the Chinese sages of old, who recognised in people related to this section of the zodiac, some of the Rat's good and bad qualities.

First and foremost the Rat is a charmer. Male and female Rats alike are affable, intelligent and disarming. When it comes to getting things done in a practical sense, like the rodent whose name they have inherited, both Mr and Miss Rat can be guaranteed to work out any problem in double quick time and come up with what is usually an ingenious solution. You can't miss these endearing and disarming types, especially at a party or any other social gathering. They will be the ones holding court in the midst of the room. Comfortable in just about any sort of company and able to discourse, interestingly if not always knowledgeably, on any subject under the sun.

Tremendous energy attends every action of this quick-witted character, together with versatility and a speculative turn that makes the Rat probably the most instinctive gambler in the Chinese zoo. Not that this always turns out to be a positive attribute of course, for the Rat can be a regular loser, even if it is capable of making spectacular gains too.

Although the Rat can talk to all manner of people, you will find him or her most at home in the company of individuals who they have come to trust implicitly; and once you gain the confidence of the Rat, there is virtually no limit to the amount of effort that will be put in on your behalf. The Rat cares little for what other people think and will support you through thick and thin if it really takes a shine to you. If, on the other hand, you are less well starred on the Rat's list of intimates, you may need to be a little more careful, because this creature is very manipulative, not always entirely ethical and is definitely willing to put one over on you if it proves possible to do so. The Rat looks after itself and those it takes to as well, if not better, than any of its animal counterparts and cares very deeply for its family.

THE RAT GOOD AND BAD

There is little doubt that, on first meeting, you will come to understand why the Rat is such a born survivor, because it is within the scope of this creature to tease, wheedle and coerce at every turn in the quest to achieve its objectives. Of course this quality could be listed as either good or bad, dependant on the situation, though there is rarely any intended malice about the Rat, even if you are deliberately duped by one, it's simply the way that he or she plays the game of life.

Be introduced to the Rat for the first time and you will find just about the most interesting character possible, and any problem only seems to come further down the line, for the Rat is also quite opinionated, unwilling to give ground when certain and resentful of doing so even when there is an element of doubt. It isn't always easy to know what the Rat might be thinking, so you could be forgiven for wondering if, behind the smile and perhaps also the back, there might be just the tiniest knife that could be thrust between your shoulder-blades at any moment. Despite this, Rats are not overtly aggressive in a physical sense - with so much cunning they don't need to be!

Rats are inclined to put their shirt on the next horse in almost any race, and though they do have a knowing knack of being able to pick winners quite regularly, there is always the danger that their luck could run out, and this is the time that the Rat becomes panicy, and perhaps a little dangerous. In business, or when it comes to the necessities of life, the Rat will fight tenaciously to stay on top. Rats like the good things in life and certainly do not like being deprived of anything that they consider to be their birthright.

If a friendly Rat comes round for a cuppa, you may need to hide the biscuits as this character is greedy. Few people remain ignorant for very long as to the general faults and failings of the rodent, though because he or she is also congenial, generous and romantic, you might be willing to send out for more chocolate digestives rather than to worry too much about such minor flaws. What really counts is a great affability and a willingness to learn by experience, something that makes the Rat-person seem all the more human, and a quality that makes any bad points within the Rat nature less difficult to forgive.

THE WORKING RAT

We are looking here at one of the most versatile little animals under the sun. Consider for a moment just how many ways and in what varied circumstances the Rat is able to gain itself a living. And so it is with the Chinese personification of the human rodent. You may have bought your last car from a Rat, or the washing machine, the stereo, that knife that is guaranteed to last forever etc., etc. Yes, the Rat is an extremely accomplished salesperson, and the adage,'I must believe in what I sell' doesn't need to apply at all here, which may be the reason that the car was missing a spare wheel, or why the knife fell to pieces the first time you cut a slice of bread with it.

Some Rats choose a career that involves helping other people, because after all there is great generosity here too. Even in the field of serving humanity however, there has to be something in it for the Rat personally, even if it is only the chance to make circumstances twist and turn just the way that the rodent really wants them to go. Don't be fooled though, because although this character knows that it has a selfish streak, it could be that it is merely being more honest than the rest of us in recognising the fact!

Boredom could be something of a problem, so it isn't likely that you would find the Rat acting as a slave to a conveyor belt, Repetition is definitely out for the archetypal Rat, whose greatest delight lies in a new challenge every five minutes. Rats are good at public relations, and excel anywhere that resourcefulness is needed. All love to feel wanted in their chosen career and would soon fly from a situation that meant working for an ungrateful employer.

Here we have quite a complex character, and one that is probably at its best in some sort of self-employment, or at the very least in a job that means plenty of decision making without recourse to senior colleagues. The Rat does not care for being told what to do and visibly wilts when subjected to criticism. Many Rats can hold down more than one job at once and may, for example, take on a bar job in the evenings; not so much for the money, but to socialise and get paid for it too! On those occasions when it becomes possible to mix business with pleasure, the Rat is certainly in his or her element, especially if enjoyment attends both.

LIFE WITH THE RAT

Life with the Rat is sometimes a little like having the Lone Ranger around: 'A flash of light, a speeding horse and a hearty Hi-ho Silver...', you know the sort of thing, out in time for the disco, leaving a pile of dirty washing and one or two half finished chores for someone else to finish. All the same, the Rat is a kind-hearted beast, so you may be off to dance the night away too - that is if you have the energy to keep up the pace.

Chances are that with a Rat in the family you will eat well, even if not everything on the table could be said to be nutritionally well-balanced. The Rat has very catholic tastes, can be a real glutton and often prefers quantity to quality. He or she will be happy to help out in the kitchen, that is if they ever stay around long enough to put on a pinny. They will not be enamoured at being left with all the routine chores of domestic life however, for in the home, as everywhere else, variety is the thing.

If you are in love with a Rat, then there are definitely two sides to the coin of relationships for you. Your rodent will always be interesting and entertaining, should be as loyal as the day is long and is very unlikely to wander far from your side. It is important that you are willing to rush hither and thither at the drop of a hat however, as the spouse does not take at all kindly to being kept waiting.

Your Rat spouse is capable of being extremely romantic, is sensual, sexy and loves variety in all things. Female Rats especially love to tease and can be guaranteed to keep the more intimate aspects of a relationship alive. If interest should wane on your part, your rodent-romeo is certain to notice at once and is likely to do whatever he or she can to redress the balance.

Many of the less acceptable sides of the Rat nature will not be seen by those who are favoured by its deep and enduring love, which extends to family members, chosen friends and, of course, other perfect and charming Rats, who are especially favoured. Although the Rat is able to find a point of reference with almost any of the other Chinese Animals, the Rat responds particularly well to the company of its own sign.

RAT COMPATIBILITY

Take a look at the table below to see how the Sign of the Rat fares in general relationships with other inhabitants of the Chinese Cosmic Zoo. The Maximum score for perfect harmony is 8.

RAT + RAT	*= 7*	*RAT + OX*	*= 7*
RAT + TIGER	*= 4*	*RAT + RABBIT*	*= 6*
RAT + DRAGON	*= 8*	*RAT + SNAKE*	*= 6*
RAT + HORSE	*= 1*	*RAT + GOAT*	*= 4*
RAT + MONKEY	*= 8*	*RAT + ROOSTER*	*= 5*
RAT + DOG	*= 6*	*RAT + PIG*	*= 6*

THE RAT AND HEALTH

Despite their apparent ability to cope with almost any circumstances, Rats are really quite vulnerable in a number of ways. In fact their up-front and sometimes over-chatty nature betrays a generally nervy quality that is all too easily pushed over the edge by continual stress or worry. It is most advantageous for the Rat to undertake some sort of meditation on a regular basis, in order to still the mind and to allow stretched nerves to snap back into place.

Worst of all for the Rat is a tendency to obesity, usually in middle and later life. This podginess is generally due to the Rat's proclivity for eating too much. A diet of cheeseburgers and chips is all too often the norm, together with cakes, puddings and chocolate bars. The correct height to weight ratio is desirable, for if anything the natural state of the Rat is slim and streamlined. Training the rodent-person to eat properly is no easy task, so the determination must come from within. Try the reverse of flattery because Rats are vain and will not want to lose their sex-appeal.

The sign of the Rat probably owes some allegiance to the kidneys, so it is quite important for Rat people to drink plenty of good, clean, and if possible untreated, water. This cleans the kidneys and allows the body to purge impurities; an important factor to any sign, though to the Rat especially.

牛

1901
1913
1925
1937
1949
1961
1973
1985
1997

IF I WANT YOU!!!

The Ox

ABOUT THE OX

The Ox, or Buffalo, is a bovine creature, and it is all too easy in the case of this apparently sedate, grazing animal, to assume that what you see is what you get. In fact, nothing could be further from the truth because the Ox is an extremely powerful beast, content enough it's true to be left alone, but quite prepared to defend itself, or members of its herd, with great strength and tenacity if it is provoked in any way. The Ox's human counterpart reflects these bovine tendencies in almost every respect. Reserved, practical and inflexible are all adjectives equally applicable in this case to human or beast.

Those born in the year of the Ox, or enjoying an Ox Rising or Moon sign, can be expected to plan almost every aspect of life in meticulous detail. You won't find this character willing to put up with any nonsense, and if you have any sense you will avoid getting in the way of an angered Ox. This is a dangerous animal, or person, because there is strength, endurance and almost blind determination.

As a parent, or an employer, the Ox can come across as an old fashioned authoritarian at times. Nevertheless there is great concern for home, family and lover, because in many respects the Ox is an old softy and wants to put a protective arm around the whole world. In more intimate, romantic situations the Ox, male or female, is slow to get moving, being naturally apprehensive and not anxious to make what might seem to be an insensitive or clumsy approach. Fortunately, once feeling secure and safe within a relationship, the Ox is certain to warm up considerably.

In all aspects of life, caution is the middle name of the Ox, which is one of the reasons why he or she is so good in business. The Ox can often be found in situations of authority, where it is recognised for its practical skills and great common sense. Whilst it could be said that there are aspects of the solid, plodding Ox that other, more gregarious, types could find to be distinctly dull, there is also application beyond belief here, not to mention the foundation of a fortune built on hard work, solid ideas and an irrepressible desire to succeed. The Ox should never be underestimated because it is almost always able to come up trumps. Few people would realise just how much potential success lies within calm, quiet Ox people.

THE OX GOOD AND BAD

Good points are not hard to find when looking at the Ox, particularly when considering the sign's ability to watch, wait and then move slowly towards its chosen objectives in life. In family life the bovine plodder promises great security and a steadfast preference for old-fashioned values. Relatives and friends alike are likely to benefit from the Ox's ability to see the most successful path for all those with whom it comes into contact. The Ox is generally kind to those it takes to and has a natural practicality to match any other animal in the Chinese zodiac.

It is the nature of life that there is always two sides to any situation however, and this is certainly the case with what must be the steadiest of careful natures. You cannot shift the irremovable, and that is exactly what the Ox is inclined to be once its mind is made up to any particular course of action. Here is stubborness on a grand scale, added to which is perseverance, often to the point of lunacy. On occasions more flexible types will leave the Ox standing, simply because this lumbering giant finds it impossible to change direction in midstream.

The Ox is a great sulker if things do not go as it would wish; brooding and petulant, and on many occasions inflexible and ridiculously over- cautious. Tell an Ox that it is facing personal disaster as a result of faulty thinking and you are likely to be told, albeit very politely, to mind your own business. The Ox will brook no interference and insists on following its own course no matter what. If faced by what it sees as signs of mutiny at home or at work, the Ox can be a bullying tyrant.

At his or her very worst, and particularly when life becomes threatening, the Ox individual can be very aggressive. This is a runaway flywheel of grand proportions, damaging everything and everyone in its path, and not an individual that many would be brave enough to cross. Thank goodness that such an extreme situation is a very rare occasion, Indeed, in some cases it may never show at all, because fortunately it is often easier to simply sit and chew the cud. Only when under repeated assault or great stress would the more aggressive qualities of this sign show themselves and it is fair to suggest that even some of the other less desirable traits of the sign are often submerged beneath a layer of affability.

THE WORKING OX

Look at any documentary film on agriculture in the Far East and you will see the patient, steady Ox, plodding its way sedately and relentlessly up and down the oriental furrows, as its ancestors have done for thousands of years. The parallel with the human Ox is all too obvious, because it isn't by sudden flashes of inspiration and blazing insights that the Ox creates one success after another in business, but rather by the same relentless, sensible plodding that is so reminiscent of the Ox's animal counterpart.

In fact the human Ox is capable of becoming involved in almost any sort of business, subjecting it to the close scrutiny and patient observation that comes as second nature. Having established the best way to go about improving things, the Ox sets to with a will, teasing and prodding any operation into shape, until it runs like clockwork.

Here we have the born organiser, and it is within the field of business that the observer is most likely to see a display of the bovine aggression that the Ox is likely to keep under wraps on most other occasions. Few could get up early enough in the day to pull the wool over this character's eyes, and people who have crossed swords with the Ox previously wouldn't dream of trying to do so again.

Humble origins are no stumbling block, and many an Ox who started life delivering papers or running errands, has ended up owning a string of companies. Perhaps unfortunately, the degree of commitment necessary to achieve such a personal coup is something that the Ox also expects from its employees, failing to recognise that we are not all made the same way. Actually stopping the Ox working is the hardest job of all. Male and Female alike, the Ox rarely takes a break and even a vacation is often endured rather than enjoyed. The problem is that to this bovine bulldozer, work is not a means to an end but rather an end in itself. When retirement finally beckons and the human Ox is put out to grass, he or she will spend the next ten years working out how to grow a bigger, lusher and more profitable crop! It's fairly common to come across Ox people who simply refuse to retire at all, though where it is imperative, you may find a somewhat subdued Ox, for what is this sign's life without a challenge?

LIFE WITH THE OX

Probably more than with any other animal in the Chinese menagerie, the possibility of getting along well with the Ox is dependant on the personality of the individual on the receiving end. Most people are able to mellow and modify their nature, the better to accommodate the peculiarities of those in their vicinity, but this is certainly not the case with the Ox.

Once the Ox loves, it is likely to be for life, though there is a difference between protecting and stifling, a fact that Mr and Miss Buffalo find difficult to take on board. For this reason the Ox is most likely to link up romantically with someone who has a preference for an almost constant protective arm around their shoulder, in which case the union may well be blessed with life-long success. Change is something that the Ox finds difficult to deal with however and any alterations in character on the part of its partner, particularly a search for personal freedom or independence, is likely to be greeted with reproachful looks and brooding silences.

The Ox makes an excellent parent, the more so if it is possessed of children who are willing to tow the line and who respect the security of a stricter than average upbringing. The Ox will arrange all the details of its offspring's education, help with the tiring routines of looking after the family and will spend considerable amounts of time patiently educating, encouraging and cajolling in equal proportion. Some difficulties may arise when the chicks want to fly the nest though, for the Ox finds it extremely difficult to let go.

So many times when people talk about a relative who is born under the influence of the Ox, you will find them saying: "Well he/she is really a very kind and caring person; but........". It's the proviso that gives the Ox away, and it comes about because the Ox not only knows how it should live its own life but thinks it has the monopoly on happiness for everyone else too. This preference for interfering is one of the traits that can make Ox people particularly difficult to get on with on occasions. This can be a distinct problem to more progressive and adventurous signs. However, it is possible that you may have already forgiven your Ox his or her idiosyncrasies. After all their concern is only born out of love, and you can't really fault anyone for that!

OX COMPATIBILITY

Take a look at the table below to see how the Sign of the Ox fares in general relationships with other inhabitants of the Chinese Cosmic Zoo. The Maximum score for perfect harmony is 8.

OX + RAT	*= 7*	*OX + OX*	*= 6*
OX + TIGER	*= 3*	*OX + RABBIT*	*= 6*
OX + DRAGON	*= 6*	*OX + SNAKE*	*= 8*
OX + HORSE	*= 5*	*OX + GOAT*	*= 1*
OX + MONKEY	*= 4*	*OX + ROOSTER*	*= 8*
OX + DOG	*= 3*	*OX + PIG*	*= 5*

THE OX AND HEALTH

Many Ox people consider themselves to be almost indestructible and it is true that this sign is inclined in the main to rude good health. Although often tending to be above average in stature, the Ox doesn't generally overeat, except during times of extreme stress, can get by on the natural exercise inherent to its regimes and is inclined to stay away from unnecessary drugs and stimulants.

The Ox fares best on an almost totally vegetarian diet, neither needing nor generally demanding large quantities of meat. The Ox lives most comfortably in a rural setting and often needs more genuine rest than it is likely to give itself the credit for requiring. Any form of limitation imposed from outside can easily make the Buffalo type dispirited and liable to all manner of maladies, and yet when the pressure comes willingly, and from within, deprivation of any sort seems to be endured comfortably and willingly.

Weak points in the constitution are apt to be the legs, and especially the area around the knees. Exercise away from the routines of work will help to keep the Ox alert fit and supple, for rheumatism and arthritis could well be a possible drawback in later life. Healthy exercise is also an important factor, though difficult to achieve for this most sedentary of signs, since the Ox would always prefer to be lazy if at all possible.

虎

NORTH POLE

1902
1914
1926
1938
1950
1962
1974
1986
1998

The Tiger

ABOUT THE TIGER

Wild and free, it is impossible ever to fully tame the Tiger, which even after many years in captivity can turn on and maim, or even kill its keeper. Part of the reason is the Tiger's unpredictability, a trait which it holds in common with its human counterparts. Of course, the similarity doesn't end here; both sorts of Tigers have a tremendous love of freedom, each is courageous, quick and intrepid.

The human Tiger is a person apart, and it takes a great deal of probing and more than a little intuition before it would be possible to announce, with any truth, that you really know one. Originality seems to be the key, some would say to the point of being deliberately different. There is no doubt that the Tiger revels in his or her ability to keep the world guessing, and most of these felines also have a distinct preference for their own company. The latter is something of a paradox, since the Tiger is also capable of being very socially minded. In some ways this aspect of the nature could be considered a 'front', probably one of the reasons why the Tiger makes such a splendid actor or actress.

The Tiger is not only a very refined person, who loves nothing more than a night out at the ballet or theatre, but is also quite creative in his or her own right. A love of music is often evident and many Tigers are also excellent at fine art or sculpture. The home of the feline is apt to be tasteful, stylish and yet genuinely original. Regular alterations in decor do not reflect a respect for trends, but are more a sign of the Tiger's need to ring the changes. Miss Tiger especially, is immaculate in her own right, as well as being liberated, independent and even radical on occasions.

All Tigers have deep humanitarian instincts and can often be found slaving away on behalf of the poor or politically downtrodden of the world. Others will be found forging a path through uncharted wastes or perhaps being the first to cross the Atlantic in an eggcup. The need to do the extraordinary is almost second-nature to the Tiger, a fact that is just as important on an intellectual level as it is with regard to the more physical aspects of life. Whatever might be considered to be different in life is meat and drink to the very original, free thinking and independent Tiger.

TIGER GOOD AND BAD

It isn't hard to find the good points of this over-sized pussycat. For starters all Tigers are beautiful, which in some way is true of their human counterparts, who exhibit a sort of magnetism that will be noticed by everyone they come into contact with. Being natural reformers, they can work tirelessly for projects that they truly believe in, happy in the knowledge that their expertise may benefit someone. Male and female Tigers alike show a reverence for, and an understanding of politics, are often liberal by inclination and can show tremendous consideration for the underdog in any given situation.

The basic problem with this striped feline lies in its overwhelming love of personal choice, so that whilst the Tiger may have all the charity and reforming zeal in the world, you are likely to wake up one morning to find that the cat has changed its mind, clothes, political beliefs, etc., etc. Yes, the Tiger does care about the world, of this there is no doubt, but there is every reason for believing that it cares for its own wellbeing more in the end.

Tigers are not always especially careful of their own best interests and so could hardly be expected to pay too much attention to what other people might believe. This may be one of the reasons that other zodiac animals find the Tiger a little difficult to deal with on occasions. What is more, the Tiger is very opinionated, so that although somewhat reckless in its approach to life, this animal knows what it believes and will not be talked round once its mind is set on a particular course. This can make the Tiger appear to be more than a little selfish and is another manifestation of the fierce independence of the animal, which can be either a blessing or a curse.

Whatever you think of this 'cuddle with claws', remember always that the Tiger is a member of the cat family, and like all its cousins, whenever it falls the Tiger can usually be relied upon to land on its feet. Those people who live with a Tiger individual are apt to say that life with any other sort of person would be dull by comparison, though this would not prevent some of the less positive aspects of the big cat getting on the nerves of others. For good or ill, the Tiger can be relied upon to make an impression. And let's face it; this is exactly what it wants to do!

THE WORKING TIGER

By far and away the best job of all for a Tiger must be that of a modern explorer. Spending a good part of each year giving lectures and raising capital, this individual can then turn his or her attention to several weeks or months charting unknown wastes; the perfect compromise of practicality and independence for this freedom loving member of the feline fraternity.

Unfortunately it is inevitable that some Tigers will find themselves in the sort of occupation that offers little or no opportunity for liberation. Think back to Tigers you have seen at the zoo, and their constant pacing up and down behind those bars. This is not so much a displacement activity as an outward sign of suppressed independence, for it doesn't matter how comfortable or well fed the Tiger may be, without freedom of movement it is nothing.

Tigers often gravitate towards self-employment, though frequently come unstuck as a result of an overwhelming inability to structure their daily routines. It's not that they are afraid of work, but who wants to do the same thing day in and day out, especially when there is a fascinating world out there to be experienced? Even if the Tiger succeeds admirably for a while, it can still make that one reckless decision that could spell disaster. If so, no problem, because at heart all cats are patient, and the Tiger will simply start again from scratch, as bold and free as ever.

Tigers make good sales-people, travellers and representatives, can often be found in teaching and are splendid musicians. They don't really care too much for dirty jobs and are good in any situation that requires quick thinking or courage. It may not come as a surprise to learn that Tigers form a fair percentage of the armed forces, for although in such a career the animal must accept a degree of discipline, there is also danger, adventure and comradeship galore; all aspects of life that the Tiger revels in.

Originality is the keyword here, so don't expect the Tiger to be very happy with the more menial or repetitive tasks that some of the other animal signs find easy to cope with. Adversity is certainly not a problem however, and the harder the task in store, the more likely the Tiger is to be the willing and able volunteer.

LIFE WITH THE TIGER

You really need to have a flexible attitude and a great deal of patience to endure a lifetime under the same roof as the impulsive, changeable Tiger. However, you could be in for some substantial rewards, particularly in terms of the interest and enthusiasm that this feline brings to anything that he or she embarks upon.

Romantically speaking the Tiger could come across as being a little cool on first impression. It's the same sort of apparent indifference that this animal exhibits towards other facets of its life because the Tiger is basically a loner and doesn't come down from the lofty peaks of self-dependence all that frequently. Under-pinning this apparent reserve is an emotional intensity that the world rarely sees, though one that is easily discernible to the individual who has managed to penetrate the Tiger's tough hide.

The Tiger seeks the sort of relationship that bears in mind a necessary individuality. Tiger spouses are often employed in careers that take them away from home regularly, and although loving and kind whilst they are around, the Tiger may soon display a tendency to gaze into the middle-distance, a certain sign that there is a longing for that fascinating world beyond the doorstep. At such times, the only sensible course of action is to let the cat out. No matter how hard you try, you will not tie this animal to a routine and must be content in the knowledge that it is not generally the way of the Tiger to seek emotional solace away from home. Unkind types might insist that the Tiger doesn't have the imagination to be unfaithful, though in reality it is more a case of not seeking the opportunity.

Tigers make good parents and will always do their best to look after the family from a financial and general wellbeing point-of-view. They bring an unconventional air to any home that they help to create, will not fetter either their partner or younger family members. They can spoil children terribly but are emphatic about the importance of a good education for their offspring. If you want a breath of genuine fresh-air in your life and in your home, you could do much worse than to take a Tiger into your life. Relationships may not be easy though and will need extra effort!

TIGER COMPATIBILITY

Take a look at the table below to see how the Sign of the Tiger fares in general relationships with other inhabitants of the Chinese Cosmic Zoo. The Maximum score for perfect harmony is 8.

TIGER + RAT	*= 4*	*TIGER + OX*	*= 3*
TIGER + TIGER	*= 6*	*TIGER + RABBIT*	*= 4*
TIGER + DRAGON	*= 6*	*TIGER + SNAKE*	*= 3*
TIGER + HORSE	*= 8*	*TIGER + GOAT*	*= 4*
TIGER + MONKEY	*= 1*	*TIGER + ROOSTER*	*= 5*
TIGER + DOG	*= 8*	*TIGER + PIG*	*= 7*

THE TIGER AND HEALTH

Within the confines of the Oriental human zoo, the Tiger may rank as one of the sturdier creatures. Of course, all the risk taking for which this big cat is famous can make the Tiger somewhat accident prone. Through an association with Western Astrology we might expect the Tiger to be liable to problems with the legs, and particularly the area between the hips and the knee. Tigers can also suffer with some circulatory problems from middle life on and will probably benefit from keeping warm.

The worst scenario for this feline is to be caged up in any way, Put the Tiger in a job it hates, tie it up in a marriage that is stifling or make it live a regimented 'nine to five' sort of existence, and the Tiger, male or female, will begin to exhibit all manner of ailments, both real and psychosomatic. Tigers like wide open spaces, low hills and airy places where they can feel the wind and smell the good, fresh air. They require a healthy, balanced diet and, moving away from the carnivore associations, should not enjoy a predominantly red meat diet.

Tiger people have been known to come through the most difficult and adverse circumstances without any difficulty whatsoever, and there is great endurance here to achieve feats that many would shy away from. Recovery from almost any situation is very good and Tigers generally bounce back from ill health is a short period of time.

1903
1915
1927
1939
1951
1963
1975
1987
1999

The Rabbit

ABOUT THE RABBIT

Consider the inoffensive rabbit. This creature is a mild-mannered herbivore. It has many natural enemies and has to keep a sharp eye out for predators of all kinds, both on the ground and from the air. Relatively defenceless, the Rabbit nevertheless manages to survive, utilising a mixture of cunning, camouflage and a stunning reproductive potential.

The human rabbit, as with the case of all animals in the Chinese zoo, shares some of the attributes of its animal counterpart, not least its ability to survive and even flourish in circumstances that might see bigger and braver souls going under. The Rabbit desires, and usually finds, a peaceful existence, is a refined person and enjoys a high degree of popularity.

The Rabbit does require a fair amount of interest in his or her life and will often gravitate towards situations that seem to be stimulating, only to move onto the next objective as soon as interest wanes. This can make the Rabbit seem a little aloof on occasions, though it is almost impossible to either disregard or to dislike a person who is so kind and generally quite personable. All Rabbits will soon remove themselves from situations of confrontation or aggression.

You will often find this character at home, for both Bucks and Does love to make a comfortable little abode for themselves and will go to almost any length to make their nearest and dearest happy too. This is not to infer that the human Bunny is anti-social - quite the opposite, for the Rabbit's gentle, refined humour makes this person welcome anywhere.

Don't be fooled though. Every Rabbit has a mind of his or her own, even if you are deliberately fooled into believing that here is a creature who accepts your point of view without any hesitation. Beneath the surface the Rabbit is burrowing away at your subconscious, subtly breaking down your prejudices and diplomatically bringing you round to his or her point of view. Even when it becomes obvious that you are being manipulated, it's hard to feel offended. The Rabbit person is generally an affable soul and not at all the sort of individual that most people would want to fall out with. Despite a little subterfuge, the Rabbit doesn't pretend to be a loveable character, it really is one!

RABBIT GOOD AND BAD

It might seem on first impression that the good points of this inoffensive character far outweigh its few faults. After all the Rabbit makes an attentive partner, a good friend and a stimulating companion. He or she is quite intuitive, takes delight in helping others and generally leaves an air of humour and bonhomie wherever it has been. The Rabbit likes to be liked, and so does everything in its power to sow the seeds of love, revelling in order and comfort, whilst revolting against squaller or avoidable adversity.

But even the Rabbit, like all of us, is a mixture of saint and sinner. Part of the reason that this has to be true lies in the Rabbit's very ability to be so popular, because it invariably takes the line of least resistance to achieve its aims. Thus you may find that some of that flattery and much of the apparent approval of you as a person, goes only skin deep as far as the Rabbit's real opinions are concerned. Here is a manipulator par-excellence, and one that will stop at nothing in its attempts to forge the kind of world where it can feel comfortable, secure and happy.

Even the kind of effort required to get you off your guard, and keep you off it, is only relevant for as long as you interest the Rabbit, for remember that this creature glories in change and may soon tire of what you have to offer. The Rabbit can be a terrible sensualist, becomes worrisome and vexatious when bored or threatened, and has been known to collapse under pressure when the going gets too tough. Fortunately things do not often go this far because the Rabbit has good self-defence mechanisms when they are needed.

Rabbits want to succeed in life, and are not beyond a little double-dealing when it suits their purposes. You might just be the person who is in the way, and although there is no deliberate desire to hurt another individual here, the Rabbit can be inclined to leave a string of casualties in its wake. Perhaps the real cause is a strong sense of self-preservation. After all, the Rabbit is not the most powerful person around, so realising the fact, he or she tends to compensate by being clever, sometimes a little too clever. You will realise when you have been hit by the Rabbit, even if it does feel like being swiped with nothing more offensive than a dandelion!

RABBIT IN BUSINESS

The Rabbit is certainly not a bold creature, so you may not expect to find it at the forefront of business activity. In fact this really isn't true because the Bunny is a good plodder, provided that the necessary interest in a particular project can be maintained. What is more, Rabbits, both male and female, are very adaptable and are able to ride out the storms of economic ups and downs, thanks to the very flexibility that is the hallmark of this animal sign.

Many Rabbits do opt for self employment, at which they excel if the original notion is well thought out. They make excellent partners for more dynamic characters, and even if this is the case they can usually be trusted to run things their own way in the end, with a mixture of diplomacy and gentle persuasion. This animal is a good organiser, though is likely to thrive more in a professional career because no Rabbit wants to get its hands dirty more than is absolutely necessary. Rabbits can be relied upon to manage themselves admirably in almost any company and will keep the peace in the busiest of workplaces, being just as popular with the lowliest employee as they are with the managing director.

Many Rabbits find their way into teaching, for the Bunny is admirable at imparting information, can demand a sort of affable respect and will readily come to terms with pupils of almost any age group. Failing an academic career, many Rabbits are quite happy to be at home. Unemployed Rabbits are rarely likely to be so for long, and in any case this resourceful creature can be guaranteed to keep itself busy - no matter what.

The very best position of all for the Rabbit would be in the diplomatic corps, also Does and Bucks alike can be found amongst marriage-guidance councillors, psychologists or personnel officers. The Rabbit is very refined and would be much at home behind the reception desk of a plush hotel. It is also noticeable amongst the ranks of creative people, for here we have the natural designer, artist or light-hearted writer. Rabbits like to be surrounded by enthusiastic types and will thrive best in the midst of those who have the same basic enthusiasms that motivate the Rabbit itself. This is one of the reasons why it is fairly common to find two or more Rabbit-types engaged at the same occupation.

LIFE WITH THE RABBIT

Despite the one or two drawbacks mentioned in the section about Rabbits Good and Bad, you really are lucky if you have opted for, or have been granted by circumstance, life with a cuddly Bunny. It is really hard to fall out with this character, the more so because even when the Rabbit does something that really annoys you, staying that way for very long is virtually impossible in this case.

As a lover the Rabbit is attentive and kind, adaptable to your needs and always willing and able to say the right thing at the right time. Add to this a refinement that defies any course behaviour or vulgarity, a good sense of fun and a liking for travel, and you may be getting your coat on already to go and find the nearest Rabbit to whom you can propose. Just stop in your tracks for a few moments though because all that glistens is not gold and there is an alternative side to the Rabbit as a room mate or live-in-lover that may not appear to be quite so appealing in the fullness of time.

For starters, although this animal can play Romeo or Juliet all too well, there certainly is not the constancy here 'unto death' that was the case with those star-crossed lovers of old. You will have to do your bit to keep the Rabbit interested in the relationship and must also bear in mind the promiscuity of which the human Bunny's animal counterpart is capable. Like it or not, the Rabbit is not the most faithful person around, which is no problem as long as you supply all the stimulation, mental and otherwise, that will be demanded. In addition, Rabbits can be quite tiring to have around, soon becoming depressed if life is not as fulfilling as it might be. At this time the Rabbit may not be such a good lover or flat-mate and there could be times when it might seem appropriate to say one or two words that you know you would regret in the fullness of time; such is the Rabbit's ability to annoy. The Rabbit's love of ease and comfort could come across as a lazy streak at times and, love him or her as much as you undoubtedly must, here you will find a person who genuinely expects to have the best of everything.

At least good breeding is almost endemic to this species, and to many people this on its own can be worth a great deal. Most important of all: Rabbit people need you so very much!

RABBIT COMPATIBILITY

Take a look at the table below to see how the Sign of the Rabbit fares in general relationships with other inhabitants of the Chinese Cosmic Zoo. The Maximum score for perfect harmony is 8.

RABBIT + RAT	*= 6*	*RABBIT + OX*	*= 6*
RABBIT + TIGER	*= 4*	*RABBIT + RABBIT*	*= 7*
RABBIT + DRAGON	*= 6*	*RABBIT + SNAKE*	*= 6*
RABBIT + HORSE	*= 3*	*RABBIT + GOAT*	*= 8*
RABBIT + MONKEY	*= 5*	*RABBIT + ROOSTER*	*= 1*
RABBIT + DOG	*= 7*	*RABBIT + PIG*	*= 8*

THE RABBIT AND HEALTH

At heart the rabbit is quite a nervy person and can easily be given to psychosomatic complaints of one sort or another. This is especially true in the case of the individual who, for no fault of his or her own, finds life to be stressful or restricting. Rabbits are herbivores and so their human counterparts are, usually by inclination, likely to stick to a diet composed mainly of vegetable produce. Green salads and plenty of healthy vegetables work best, whilst processed or convenience foods such as pizza and burgers may not suit this creature, unless maintained as an exception rather than as a rule.

By association with Western Astrology the Rabbit could easily suffer with ailments that affect the feet. With this regard, good footwear is essential and sensible pedicure a distinct advantage. Some association with the kidneys also seems to be evident, so it is important for the Rabbit to drink plenty of fresh, unadulterated water.

Rabbits don't like cold and damp and in winter are often to be found toasting their toes in front of a warm fire. Nevertheless it should be remembered that the Rabbit does need a fair dose of healthy exercise every day to remain healthy. This situation is not always easily achieved, thanks to an inbuilt lazy streak and a desire to do the very least that is necessary in order to live a comfortable life.

龍

1904
1916
1928
1940
1952
1964
1976
1988
2000

The
Dragon

ABOUT THE DRAGON

Even Western tales of dragons make it plain that any self-respecting knight had to have his wits about him to get the better of this fearsome beast. For their part, although the Chinese have always had a slightly softer spot for this scaly, mythical creature than has been the case in the Occident, the general character of the Dragon has remained similar.

All of this tells us a great deal about the sort of people the Chinese of old thought that they were dealing with when they named this member of the Chinese zoo, for the Dragon can be a fearsome animal, the more so when viewed through the eyes of more timorous creatures. Dragons are apt to be dominant by nature and do not care to be crossed; there is an energy and a determination here that rivals any other zodiac sign. Bold and fearless, the Dragon chooses to meet life head on, is always competitive and really does need to win.

Don't run away with the idea that this fire-breathing leftover from fairy tales always thinks things through clearly. On the contrary the Dragon is certain to have an impulsive streak, and it is one that can precipitate this overgrown lizard into heaps of trouble. While the rest of us are sizing up the next job on our personal agenda, the Dragon is already hard at work. Resilience is endemic, and at least the Dragon is capable of learning from past mistakes.

Here is not a creature given to follow anyone, it doesn't suffer fools gladly, and that can include anyone who doesn't think along the same progressive and ambitious lines. So positive is the Dragon's assertion that it knows what it is talking about, there are very few individuals who would dare to argue the point.

The Dragon is often ethical and can be a stickler for detail. There is a natural fire here, no matter what Element ruled the year of the Dragon's birth. Out and about, it should be easy enough to pick out the Dragon, especially if you find yourself near to the complaints department of a high street store. The Dragon is the person at the counter, demanding a refund or complaining about the quality of the goods. But for all the smoke and fire that attends the Dragon's arrival, you will at least know that you have a brave champion on hand. And once the Dragon takes to you, you're a friend for life.

DRAGON GOOD AND BAD

At heart the Dragon is a natural warrior and as such cannot be considered to be the most patient person you will ever meet. What tends to make matters worse is the fact that Dragons, Miss or Mr, invariably consider themselves to be in the right, even if it has been proven to them conclusively that their point of view is not valid. Here lies the greatest problem for the creature, and what underpins some of its worst traits.

Self opinionated, over-bearing and down-right bossy. These are all accusations hurled in the direction of the smoke and flames that belch from the nostrils of the reptile-king. Play anything from a game of chess to a round of golf with a Dragon and unless you are lucky you could find that you have a minor war on your hands. It wouldn't even be sensible to throw the game in the Dragon's favour either, because here we have a creature determined to win on its own merits, even if to do so might threaten its own life and limb, not to mention the end of a beautiful friendship. The Dragon is often boastful, invariably working out its next plan for running anything from a company to a country, will never, ever lose an argument and finds it almost impossible to apologise. Dynamic in a business sense, the Dragon has to be managing director and finds it very difficult to take orders from anyone. Of course there are always two sides to every coin, and for all the steam and bluster of which the Dragon is capable, there is also a basically kind person lurking behind that iron-clad skin.

You will find the Dragon to be extremely versatile and even ingenious on occasions. Although very ambitious, the Dragon can work just as hard to fund a charitable enterprise as it can to fill its own treasure-chest and is probably the most loyal of all Chinese zodiac animals. The Dragon is almost incapable of cheating at anything, can keep going when everyone else has fallen by the wayside and is a champion of the deserving underdog. Of course there are times when the underdog is happy to stay where it is, not that this will have any bearing on the behavior of the irrepressible Dragon, who having got his or her tallons into any situation finds it difficult, if not imposible to let go. This is the reson why the Dragon is often accused of being a busy-body, and could account for a slight lack of popularity on occasions.

THE WORKING DRAGON

What the Dragon needs more than anything else in life is to feel that it is in charge, which is why this animal is apt to gravitate to the top of the pile, no matter how matter-of-fact or menial the task in hand may be. The Dragon is a hard worker, always puts in more hours than anyone else is willing to do and can be guaranteed to have the best interests of his or her own company at heart.

Company managers employing a Dragon will, at first, thank their lucky stars that they have found such a versatile and conscientious employee, though it may not be very long before they begin to develop some doubts, particularly when it comes to watching their own back. The scaly reptile king has original ideas for improving most situations and can revolutionise manufacturing processes, probably decimating the work-force on the way.

It is fair to say that the Dragon is not a person to take on menial tasks, though would rather be sweeping the streets than doing nothing at all. In such an eventuality the Dragon would either design a bigger and more efficient brush, or make plans for the creation of a machine that could do the job far more efficiently; patent the device and then form a company to manufacture it. You won't find the Dragon, boss or worker, to be especially patient with more plodding types and this animal will only be truly happy when he or she has attained the key to the executive wash-room.

Dragons are good in the armed forces, after all they are naturally quite brave. Like all people they make mistakes in their work, though those of the Dragon can be epic in proportion, because if you don't take a big risk you cannot expect to be in for a gigantic profit. Yet it isn't really the thought of making money that keeps the Dragon going. Achievement is all that really matters. After the first million is made, the Dragon is already too busy making the next one to worry about spending the first. The path is always onwards and upwards, towards some elusive destination that only the Dragon person him or herself recognises. Dragons mix well with each other, though more in a social sense than in a work one. After all, there can only be one king or queen at once, and that is what the Dragon really sees itself as being. Power is all, so look out St George!

LIFE WITH THE DRAGON

Life with the Dragon, and how you take to it, depends more than ever in this case on what the relationship is and also what sort of a person you are. It isn't everyone who could cope with the manic outbursts, frequent comings and goings and workaholic proclivities of the average Dragon person. On the other hand, all of this could also infer a fairly comfortable life in other respects, especially since the Dragon is very good at making money but probably doesn't really care all that much about how it is spent.

Although capable of showing some passion in a romantic sense, it's the cut and thrust of the world beyond your front door that appeals most to the Dragon, which makes him or her less likely than some to seek fresh fields and pastures new relationship-wise. If your Dragon rings up to say that he or she will have to put in some extra hours at the office, you can be fairly certain that they are speaking the truth. It could even be suggested that all this natural aggression works against a particularly romantic inclination in any case, for the divorce rate of Dragons, on the grounds of infidelity at least, appears to be very low.

What is more to the point is whether or not you can stand to be criticised frequently, taken to task for not having the same point of view as your spouse and to be expected to be a mind-reader. If the answer to all these questions is no, then you are going to find the Dragon a rather irritating person to have around. Conversely you will have to bear in mind the element of surprise that attends life with this person. Dragons are willing to do almost anything on whim, which could include a flight to some exotic foreign locations, assuming finances and work-load allow. The Dragon is a good parent and all Dragons take their responsibilities as spouse and parent very seriously, fighting as tenaciously on account of those they love as they do regarding other aspects of life.

Much depends here on the nature of the individual who has chosen to live with the Dragon. This is not a person who relishes being contradicted or crossed in any way. The cleverest of would-be partners are aware that a degree of psychology can work wonders and keep the fire simmering in the Dragon's throat, but the flames controlled.

DRAGON COMPATIBILITY

Take a look at the table below to see how the Sign of the Dragon fares in general relationships with other inhabitants of the Chinese Cosmic Zoo. The Maximum score for perfect harmony is 8.

DRAGON + RAT	*= 8*	*DRAGON + OX*	*= 6*
DRAGON + TIGER	*= 6*	*DRAGON + RABBIT*	*= 6*
DRAGON + DRAGON	*= 7*	*DRAGON + SNAKE*	*= 7*
DRAGON + HORSE	*= 6*	*DRAGON + GOAT*	*= 6*
DRAGON + MONKEY	*= 8*	*DRAGON + ROOSTER*	*= 7*
DRAGON + DOG	*= 1*	*DRAGON + PIG*	*= 6*

THE DRAGON AND HEALTH

Considering the amount of stress that this creature constantly puts itself under, it's a wonder that the Dragon is as robust as it tends to be. It may not come as a surprise however to discover that the Dragon is subject on occasion to violent headaches and also migraine. Accumulated stress tends to take this route in the case of the Dragon because the muscles in the neck and scalp are always so tense.

Dragons are not especially careful of their diets. They are completely omnivorous, though with a preference for meat, do not tend to put on weight disproportionately and are commonly found standing in the queue at the take-away. These days 'fair damsels' do not figure amongst the Dragon's culinary preferences, though in the case of male Dragons could well stimulate their appetites in other directions. Routines can drive the reptile-king mad and like so many other of the Chinese animals the Dragon can suffer through containment or long periods of unremitting stress. On the whole, though by no means indestructible, the Dragon is usually more healthy than its lifestyle seems to deserve.

The Dragon responds very well to changes in location, so holidays at regular intervals are a must. Confusion, either of an emotional or of a practical nature should be avoided, and a steady, organised routine encouraged.

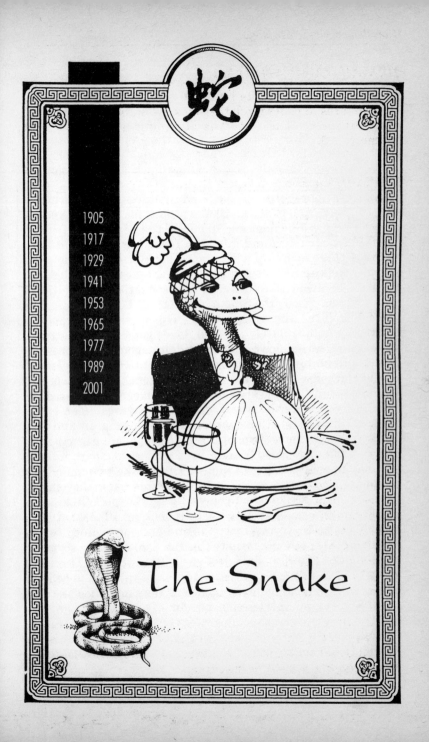

蛇

1905
1917
1929
1941
1953
1965
1977
1989
2001

The Snake

ABOUT THE SNAKE

The Snake, like its fellow creature the Rat, has generally had a bad press as far as humanity is concerned. Fortunately those inscrutable observers of nature, the Chinese magicians and astrologers of old, were not subject to the prejudices that have prevailed in other cultures. They saw much to admire in the reclusive snake, and also realised how much it had in common with certain astrological types.

On the whole snakes are reserved creatures, even retiring in some cases, and so it is with Snake people; for despite a veneer of sociability, refinement and glamour, the Serpent individual is basically a one-off and a loner. This type can spend long hours simply curled up with a good book or laid in the sunshine, travels around slowly, if at all, and takes great delight in the known rather than the new and sensational.Despite its reserved demeanour the Snake is no ascetic however, refusing to deny itself the finer things of life. This is why the serpent is invariably immaculately dressed, loves good food and drink, has a strong sexual drive and is fastidious about cleanliness.

All sensual motivations are important to the Snake, most of whom are also cultured to a greater extent than their peers. At a social function the snake will be the elegantly dressed individual, sampling the finest wines and cheeses, keen to indulge in polite social discourse, yet displaying an amiable intrigue that is almost hypnotic. Snake people are warm by nature and can make good friends, even if there is a part of them that few people ever get to know. They make extremely bad enemies because, as with the creature whose name they share, they are apt to strike when you would least expect them to do so. They are astute when it comes to looking after what they consider to be their own interests and are not inclined to pry into the lives of others. Despite this the Snake always seems to know what is going on and is not easily hoodwinked. There are many aspects to the Snake person that are inclined to be both misunderstood, and on many occasions the Snake itself is willing to actively support the situation. The reason is simple; what could be better than to keep everyone guessing? All inhabitants of the zoo would do well to look carefully towards the Reptile House and beware: it is very easy to underestimate the Snake!

SNAKE GOOD AND BAD

This person is not an individual to make any decision either lightly or quickly, so much so that a few unkind people have accused the Snake of being somewhat lazy. It really all depends on your point of view, and perhaps has something to do with either being, or not being, a snake yourself! It is true that Snakes love to lounge around, and they may even sometimes typify that wonderful quote from *Three men in a boat*. "Work? Why I adore it, I could watch it all day!" However, this should not be taken to mean that the serpent is incapable of doing its fair share of toil when necessary. Snakes are good at what takes their fancy and can work hard at routine tasks, for as long as the interest lasts.

The snake is generally very refined, so when you take him or her to the restaurant they are certain to behave themselves. They probably know more about good food and wine than you do, and in ordering are sure to charm the pants off the head waiter. All good points it has to be admitted, though the problem could come when the food does, because if there is one thing that the Snake loves, it's to eat. In fact, and not to put too fine point on it, the Snake is a glutton. The worst of the breed are sensualists to the extreme. In addition to eating to excess they spend hours in the bathroom, love to stay in bed all day and can spend a fortune on fashionable clothes. Can you forgive the snake for its hedonistic tendencies? Certainly you can, because to make up for the fact, there is a sense of mystery and intrigue here that is second to none.

The Snake is sexy, softly spoken, kind and attentive. It makes a good parent, is usually loyal and knows how to please. When it comes to bringing in the bacon the Serpent is a veritable pig-breeder. It is quite easy for the Snake to hold down a number of different jobs at the same time, if that is what it takes to live the comfortable sort of existence that this Chinese sign desires. Best of all, the charming, suave Snake knows better than any other sign how to get itself, and you, out of any kind of trouble. It can move mountains when necessary and finds it easy to persuade others to work on its behalf, even when the chips are down. The Snake is not inclined to lose control, either of itself or of any situation and is quite capable of making defeat into victory.

THE WORKING SNAKE

Snake people do not care to get their hands dirty, so it is highly unlikely that you will be greeted by a boiler-suited member of this fraternity next time you take the car in to be serviced. However, the person who greets you with a cordial smile and a polite approach in the boutique may well be a snake. This breed are often to be found in shops and service industries generally. Amongst the professions that would suit a Snake best could be listed hotel manager, restaurant owner, executive car salesman, typist, personal assistant or clerical officer. This can only be a broad cross-section because we are dealing with a very versatile type here. The main criteria is that the Snake gets on very well with people and has a quiet, trustable charm that would sell a refrigerator to an eskimo.

Most snakes have the ability to make money in one way or another and will even take on a job that really does not befit their unique qualities sooner than not have one at all. It isn't that the snake is adverse to sitting around at home with a good book, it has more to do with the fact that the Serpent needs money in order to live the sort of life that suits it the best. Snakes who do find themselves employed in some menial position can soon charm their way up the ladder of success and can be expected to maintain an elevated position once it has been achieved.

Being basically humanitarian by disposition, the Snake can also be at home amongst the ranks of nurses and doctors. There is an ability here to empathise and eventual specialisation is to be expected. The Serpent is also to be found in areas of self-employment, though may well appear to defer to a more vigorous or aggressive partner. When it comes to handling finance, the wily Snake is second to none, so if you want to make a mint on the stock exchange, you could do very much worse than to grab the tail of an ascending 'City Snake' and hang on, no matter what! It's worth realising that the Snake who takes to you is capable of being very giving, both in terms of time and money. Snakes do like to be wealthy, though more as a means to an end rather than as an end in itself. Because of this the average Snake is also happy to share what it has, both with the world at large and with any individual that it takes to.

LIFE WITH THE SNAKE

It would be difficult to imagine a more charming partner, flat-mate or adoring relative than the Snake, who is everybody's favourite aunt or uncle, a joy to be around and as pleasant as the day is long.

The Snake is possessed of a charm that is felt by almost everyone and an intrigue that makes even a long-standing life-partner want to know yet more about this most enigmatic person. Alas, there is no such thing as perfection, and though the Snake is unlikely to fill your house with loud music that you find objectionable, or leave dirty socks all over the place; you may have to invest in a second bathroom if you want to make life with this creature comfortable. Remember, the Snake is a sensualist, who can stay amongst the soap-suds for hours on end. You may also have to take a degree in cookery, because unless you are lucky enough to have a Snake who is kitchen-trained you will need to be on your culinary metal. Only the lightest of souffles and the crispest of salads will suit the Snake, who can make eating into a veritable art-form.

When it comes to going out anywhere, start the Snake on its preparations several hours in advance. Assuming you can ever get him or her away from the larder and out of the house, you should be in for a good social life. This creature loves to mix, though in an inconspicuous way, is often very good looking and would grace any arm at a social function. Being able to mix as happily with a tramp as with a member of the royal family, the Serpent appears to know something about any subject, though has the knowing ability to make everyone else feel themselves to be an expert. As for presentation, in the case of Miss Snake especially, from the top of her most coiffured curl, down to the tip of her hand-made Italian shoes, she is the epitome of sartorial elegance. And in the case of both sexes, what you find inside the wrapping is about as alluring as anyone could reasonably expect.

The Snake can become a little bad-tempered if things do not turn out as it wishes and life at such times could become a little uncomfortable. At such times a little temporary sulking could be the result, though the right sort of encouragement should return the Snake to its usual state of equilibrium in virtually no time at all.

SNAKE COMPATIBILITY

Take a look at the table below to see how the Sign of the Snake fares in general relationships with other inhabitants of the Chinese Cosmic Zoo. The Maximum score for perfect harmony is 8.

SNAKE + RAT	= 6	*SNAKE + OX*	= 8
SNAKE + TIGER	= 3	*SNAKE + RABBIT*	= 6
SNAKE + DRAGON	= 7	*SNAKE + SNAKE*	= 7
SNAKE + HORSE	= 3	*SNAKE + GOAT*	= 4
SNAKE + MONKEY	= 3	*SNAKE + ROOSTER*	= 8
SNAKE + DOG	= 6	*SNAKE + PIG*	= 1

THE SNAKE AND HEALTH

Although the snake is a fairly robust creature, the human version can on occasions be its own worst enemy. The problem lies in the Serpent's great liking for food and drink. Early in life this may not be too much of an obstacle, though with middle-age the Snake could all too easily develop a rather weighty, couch-potato type of physique. Of course carrying around too much weight can put a stress on the heart and could also incline the Snake to an ever more sedentary life-style than is really good for it.

The part of the body ruled by the sign of the Snake is the throat, another area of the Serpent's constitution that may be the focus of ill-health if a sensible life is not opted for. In terms of mental health, the Snake requires a comfortable home and freedom of movement to be at its most robust. It should be noted though that Snakes are inclined to longevity, probably partly because they are not really worrisome types by nature. Other Chinese signs could learn something important from this fact. All Reptiles tend to live for a considerable period, a fact that also has something to do in this case with the Snake's abilty to turn itself off from situations that it doesn't really care for. So what if the rest of the world fails to approve and considers the Snake to be more like an Ostrich on occasions? It's better than ending up suffering from fatigue or stress. If in doubt, stop to watch the flowers growing for a while!

馬

1906
1918
1930
1942
1954
1966
1978
1990
2002

The Horse

ABOUT THE HORSE

Fleetest of all animals in the Chinese menagerie, the horse comes breezing onto the scene with a whinny and a kick of its hind legs. This is no domesticated nag, but a wild, free creature, with which the Chinese sages of old must have been very familiar. And as always these shrewdest of observers knew exactly what they were talking about when they designated the sign of the Horse to this part of their zodiac.

Horse people have an exuberance and a love of life that is probably without parallel, they hate to be tied to one place and are at their very best when allowed to follow their own, somewhat erratic course. The best way to tame a human horse is to flatter him or her, commenting on the very real intelligence that springs from that quick brain. The Horse will find some good things to say about you too, though whether or not he or she will be saying the same things tomorrow, who can tell? The human Equine is unpredictable, capricious, flirtatious and as mercurial as they come.

With a Horse around there is a good chance that you will not lack entertainment, after all this character is the natural actor of the zodiac; a song, a dance and a wise-crack, all rolled into one. Taking life seriously for more than five minutes at a time is not easy for this individual, though he or she is possessed of an ingenuity that could baffle the steadier Ox or the more emotionally motivated Goat.

Any horse worth its salt could prove conclusively to you that black is white, and will then sell you the paint into the bargain. The Horse can solve most mental puzzles in a flash and does not find it at all difficult to perform several totally different tasks at the same time. Romance is this animal's middle name, even if it finds it a little difficult to remain constant for a protracted period. Human Horses are resourceful, willing, funny, nervy and kind. Change and variety are especially important in the lives of these individuals, who probably have a lower boredom threshold than just about any other animal in the Chinese Zoo. Conformity is not something that the average Horse person is particularly interested in and there is always a radical and different streak. Be happy if your Horse sticks around, but don't try to pin one down though, all you will see are the hoof prints in the sand.

THE HORSE GOOD AND BAD

The sense of fun that attends life when there is a Horse around will be obvious to anyone in the vicinity. This animal is a talker, guaranteed to enliven the dullest of gatherings and always interesting. Unfortunately, stimulating though the discourse may be, there is no certainty that the Horse has any real idea what he or she is actually talking about. This is the unwitting con-man of the zodiac, not evil or even intent on doing any harm, but spreading confusion and sometimes dissension wherever he or she goes.

The greatest accusation levelled at the Horse is that it has such a butterfly mind, and is inclined to start a new task before the last one has been finished. Whilst this is true to a certain extent, it has to be remembered that Mr or Miss Horse is usually quite capable of dealing with a number of situations simultaneously and, with application, can handle most of them very well. Enthusiasm is always present, no matter what the task in hand may be, but fools rush in where angels fear to tread, and there is little doubt that the Horse is considered to be number one fool in the Chinese zoo. A search for continuity is important, in thinking as well as in doing, but after all there is so much in the world to see and do, and the Horse doesn't want to miss any of it.

The Horse loves to have a good time, and wants you to have one too. There could be a problem here, particularly since the Equine person finds it difficult, if not impossible, to understand that your mind might work in a different way and that you may decide to do your own thing. If thwarted in their endeavours, Horses can become cantankerous and nervy; they are unique in character, almost to the point of being down-right eccentric and will allow nobody to interfere in their lives.

There is nothing deliberately malevolent in the average Horse's behaviour, but that does not prevent difficulties and even sometimes disasters attending the lives of those with whom they come into contact. Often this is brought about as a result of a misunderstanding as to what the Horse actually is and what its needs in life may really be. More than with any other sign it is good for people who mix with the Horse type to know in advance what they should expect. After all, knowing is half way to controlling!

THE WORKING HORSE

The Horse is a born communicator, and it is vitally important that this fact is taken into account whatever career may be chosen. In the wild, the Horse is a herd animal, and its human counterpart is not so very different. This is why the horse is best when working in any group situation, where ideas can be bounced around, altered, modified and ultimately put into action. The world of advertising, those of journalism, public relations and sales, all sport a fair number of Horse types. The Horse is also to be found in counselling situations, for it is a good listener as well as a talker.

What the Horse hates most of all is to be tied to any sort of inflexible routine, so you won't often find this person feeding a conveyor belt or painting the beaks on plastic ducks. However, when it comes to thinking up an ingenious way to assist others to perform such tasks in a more efficient way, the Horse is in its element. Ideas are the thing, and as long as the Horse is able to express these, together with its unique personality, you will have a contented nag on the payroll.

Where the Horse takes the option of self-employment, things work out best when it can form a partnership with some less gregarious and slightly more ordered type, to steady down the Equine enthusiasm and to make certain that the books are kept. Details are of no real importance to the Horse, who simply wants to get on and do whatever is necessary to bring in the bacon. Piles of paper to be dealt with would be inclined to send the Horse galloping off into the sunset, whilst even the threat of boredom is enough to make the horse scan the pages of situations vacant for a more rewarding career. This is a person who could enjoy more than one career in his or her working life, and the changes between them can be very radical. Confidence to make a fresh start is rarely lacking, nor the intelligence necessary to do so. Horse people will often go on with one form of education or another late into middle-age; they can never learn enough to please themselves, are ideal material for re-training and love a challenge.

The horse, no matter how settled it may be in its career, is always happy to hear the evening buzzer sound; for to this gregarious and life-loving creature work is a means to an end and not an end in itself.

LIFE WITH THE HORSE

For the right kind of person, life with the Horse can be a totally enlivening and eventful experience. For one thing the Horse is almost guaranteed to keep you laughing; it doesn't take life all that seriously itself and is in any case the natural joker in the Chinese pack. Beware though, because the Horse can be very disorganised, will leave dirty washing all over the place and if it decides to cook a meal may leave the kitchen looking like the aftermath of a medieval battle.

In an emotional sense this creature is a fickle character, can be a dreadful flirt, but will usually remain faithful if he or she gets the stimulation from you that is so necessary to keep the Horse happy and content. You won't find this Nag to be a nag, that is unless you fail to be ready immediately when it's time to go out and trip the light-fantastic. This could be a frequent occurrence, and not always at a time when you are feeling at your best. If the Horse decides to stay up and boogy all night, and this is a distinct possibility, you will be expected to prop your eyelids open with a couple of matches and join in.

The Equine human is given to excesses of all kinds and rarely keeps still for more than a few minutes at a time. You might try getting him or her involved in a good book however, as this is just about the only thing, short of absolute exhaustion, that will keep the horse tied to the same spot for two consecutive hours.

Being kind, and in the main considerate of your feelings, the Horse can be a true romantic, even if it forgets about you the moment that something, or someone, more stimulating comes along. This is an infuriating, loveable rogue of the zodiac; a perpetual child who makes an admirable parent, simply because it has forgotten to grow up itself. The average Horse Mum or Dad is not content to pack the kids off for a picnic, but rather will seek to make every small outing into and adventure of 'Swallows and Amazons' proportions. And when it comes to a new train set at Christmas, it's highly likely that any children around would have to wait until well into Boxing day before they got a look in. As a lover the Horse maintains a sense of the immediate that prevents things from becoming stale, so that life with the Horse can be difficult at times but is never, ever dull.

HORSE COMPATIBILITY

Take a look at the table below to see how the Sign of the Horse fares in general relationships with other inhabitants of the Chinese Cosmic Zoo. The Maximum score for perfect harmony is 8.

HORSE + RAT	= 1	*HORSE + OX*	= 5
HORSE + TIGER	= 8	*HORSE + RABBIT*	= 3
HORSE + DRAGON	= 6	*HORSE + SNAKE*	= 3
HORSE + HORSE	= 7	*HORSE + GOAT*	= 7
HORSE + MONKEY	= 4	*HORSE + ROOSTER*	= 5
HORSE + DOG	= 8	*HORSE + PIG*	= 6

THE HORSE AND HEALTH

In its earliest years the Horse really is too busy to be bothered for long at a time by ill-health, though Horses can suffer with many minor childhood diseases. It really is in later life that problems are likely to emerge, and for a number of reasons. For starters the Horse simply does not know how to rest, and this can lead to nervous as well as physical exhaustion. It is all too easy for the Equine individual to become hooked on tobacco or alcohol, both parts of the social scene that the Horse relishes; and these too could take their toll eventually.

Ideally, the Horse should live in the country, take plenty of fresh air and enjoy a well-balanced and nutritious diet. In reality none of these considerations are likely to figure prominently until at least some damage has already been done. However, it might be suggested that one of the most important components of health, probably the most significant, is a proclivity for happiness. In this department the Horse tends to win out, rarely being without a smile for long at a time. And it's true that the happy-go-lucky and carefree Horse is usually bouncing with health and vitality. Worry is a definite irritant however and should be avoided at all cost. Perhaps most Horse types would find this difficult as they are worriers by nature. However, a combination of meditation and relaxation might help.

1907
1919
1931
1943
1955
1967
1979
1991
2003

The Goat

ABOUT THE GOAT

Goats, and especially wild ones, are not especially easy to approach, and will invariably head for the hills at the first sign of an approaching stranger. This at least reflects part of the mental attitude displayed by the human Goat, though it has to be said that the similarities inherent here between animal and human are not so well defined as in the case of other Chinese signs.

It isn't in terms of social niceties that you will find the Goat to be ill-at-ease or inclined to avoid your company. On the contrary the Goat, male or female, is fairly sociable, at least on a superficial level. But once the trivialities are over, the Goat will be anxious to turn the conversation in your direction, mainly because these people have a desire to keep many aspects of their own nature a closely guarded secret. The Goat is, nevertheless, cultured and refined, takes delight in fine- art, literature and the company of intellectual types, and will unburden that deep mind, though only when the recipient is known thoroughly and trusted absolutely.

The Goat can be something of a sensualist, a fact that displays itself in a number of ways. There is a love of good food and drink, and an extravagance when it comes to buying clothes or personal adornments. Despite this, the Goat really cares very little for materialistic considerations and could easily live on a desert island, where the requirements of sensual fulfilment may be no further away than the nearest sleepy lagoon, with its warm sands and coconut palms.

The average Goat is naturally lucky, can be dedicated to a cause it feels strongly about but is likely to be dreadfully insecure, particularly so about relationships. Getting on with others is something that can be a problem to this creature and it is likely to have many acquaintances though few real friends. You could work alongside a Goat for months or years, without really ever getting to know what makes him or her tick as a human being. Both Mr and Miss Goat can be equally difficult to get to know, their natural reserve acting as a sort of a shell to protect them from what they often see as a threatening world. Despite this reserve however, once this individual learns to love, it does so ardently and, true to the nature of the Goat, usually for life.

GOAT GOOD AND BAD

This is one Chinese animal that has a number of undeniably attractive features and it is difficult to imagine finding a truly difficult member of the species. The Goat will always do its best to help you out if you are in trouble. This is a trait that usually holds good on a personal level, though in the case of some situations the Goat takes on more of the persona of the Ostrich, burying its head in the sand rather than facing up to the harsh realities of life. This course of action is directly related to sensitivity and not to a lack of concern. The sight of starving children or wounded animals on the television screen is deeply painful to the soft-hearted Goat. Since these are situations beyond its own control, it would rather pretend that they did not exist.

Goats are very creative, often making fine artists themselves. Taking this natural flair for making things look good, they can also arrange situations, and in the case of the cleverer ones, people too! This is done in a spirit of genuine concern, so that even here it is difficult to talk about selfish motives in the case of this most unusual of people. The Goat is more responsive than most Chinese signs to the elementary principle that sets a seal on what can be a fairly neutral nature, though whatever the element, cross or annoy the Goat at your peril, for it has a long memory. Sexually motivated, the Goat can easily manipulate others with this natural proclivity for yet another facet of its sensuality. But don't be fooled, the Goat is not promiscuous, so there may be a price to pay.

Often the very gentility of this animal sign is the start of the observer's undoing. All that glistens may not be gold, so don't be fooled into thinking that the Goat is a soft-touch. Goats fight tenaciously for what they see as being their own and make stern enemies indeed, once that deep nature is really troubled or threatened.

As surely and certainly as the animal whose name they have taken, the human Goat individual can climb high mountains, jump wide chasms in its search for what it wants most from life. It may take several decades to find its destination, but it will not brook your interference and is certain to bear a grudge if you really afford it an emotional injury of any sort whilst it is looking.

THE WORKING GOAT

The Goat is a happy, flexible and capable worker. This part of the Chinese zodiac is fairly adaptable and so is likely that you might encounter the Goat in almost any sort of employment. However there are preferences; for example the Goat is a rather cultured creature and would be at its happiest in a career that allowed the artistic sensitivity to find an outlet. Goats make good artists in their own right, would be ideal in interior design, draughtsmanship, window dressing and similar careers, where a deft touch and a good eye are essential.

It isn't especially necessary for the Goat to be a high-flyer, on the contrary you are more likely to find this character at his or her best as a second-in-command, rather than as the General. This is part of the reason why the Goat makes a splendid secretary or personal assistant. In the case of either job, not only intelligence and know-how are necessary but also an ability to look good. The Goat has all these qualities, and can also bring a light-hearted and homely feel to any workplace, no matter how busy or impersonal it may be. The Goat always wants to please, and perhaps a little too much sometimes, so don't be surprised if this person goes on and on until they are exhausted, probably then taking some days to recover.

Female Goats, and many male ones too, have a mothering instinct, which is why they are often to be found in careers that involve caring for others. Nursing, geriatric work or psychology are all possibilities, and the Nanny-Goat is often quite happy to make her life at home, running the house and looking after the children, which to this animal can become a career in itself. There is no doubting though that the happiest Goats of all are those who work at, or close to, home. This may seem something of a paradox, as the Goat is a good traveller, in fact probably the best roamer of them all but being close to its roots in a daily sense helps to prevent the onset of insecurity which is the hallmark of this astrological type.

Should the Goat fail to establish the sort of home surroundings that suit it so well, either as a result of a difficult childhood or possibly because of problems later in life, the thwarted Goat may throw itself into its work to the exclusion of all else.

LIFE WITH THE GOAT

When it comes right down to it, relationships of a deeply personal type have a great deal to do with the psychological needs of the respective participants, and this is especially true in the case of the Goat. Of course, if you are living with a Goat by way of kinship, or have one as a flat-mate, the situation is different, but where intimacy is the key, the Goat has some very unique needs.

Male Goats are usually on the lookout for a mother-figure, which in some peculiar way matches the nurturing tendencies within their own nature. As with she-Goats they are attentive partners, kind and in the main understanding, though possessed of a desire to feel that they are loved absolutely. The Goat needs a protective arm around its shoulder and can soon become insecure if this is not forthcoming, or is withdrawn with the passing of time. Miss Goat especially is often viewed as a sexual time-bomb, just waiting for the right person to come along and light the fuse. All Goats are liberated in their attitude towards personal relationships and tend towards highly physical encounters.

In terms of everyday life, you should find the Goat to be an easy-going sort of character. They like to have a tidy, well routined and attractive home, make excellent parents and can be guaranteed to fulfil their responsibilities. Goats also love to travel, especially by water, and are not stick-in-the-mud types when it comes to change of any sort, just as long as they can go on feeling secure and safe with their partner. This aspect of the Goat cannot be overstated, for though this creature could make its home in a tent on the side of an active volcano if necessary, the most important aspect of all is that the Goat needs to feel at home, which is more a case of psychological need than it is of matching decor or bone-china crockery.

Goats can be very intrepid, and it may have been this breed that followed the Nile to its source or first explored the rain-forests of Borneo; so keen are they to forge new paths in the world that there is virtually no lengths to which they would not go. On the way, people in the plural are not especially important, but wherever the Goat does set its intrepid step it will almost certainly take a live-in lover along for security and company.

GOAT COMPATIBILITY

Take a look at the table below to see how the Sign of the Goat fares in general relationships with other inhabitants of the Chinese Cosmic Zoo. The Maximum score for perfect harmony is 8.

GOAT + RAT	*= 4*	*GOAT + OX*	*= 1*
GOAT + TIGER	*= 4*	*GOAT + RABBIT*	*= 8*
GOAT + DRAGON	*= 6*	*GOAT + SNAKE*	*= 4*
GOAT + HORSE	*= 7*	*GOAT + GOAT*	*= 7*
GOAT + MONKEY	*= 4*	*GOAT + ROOSTER*	*= 4*
GOAT + DOG	*= 3*	*GOAT + PIG*	*= 8*

THE GOAT AND HEALTH

The Goat is a generally robust creature and suffers relatively little ill health, though more so than with any human-creature in the Chinese zoo, so much depends on the emotional state of the Goat when it comes to assessing physical health. At heart the Goat is a worrier, not so much about paying the gas bill or making certain that the mortgage is up-to-date, but more about the state of relationships, and even concerning the wider world beyond the Goat's own door.

If allowed to get out of control, emotional upsets of any sort can create nervous tension in the Goat, which can be reflected particularly in gastric problems, together with general debility.

The Goat needs to feel that everything is as it should be, even if this means hanging on grimly in the face of adversity. To the Goat it is not the state of play that counts, but knowing the score. Goats should therefore strive for a settled life and should not allow fatigue or nervous tension to build up more than is absolutely necessary. Healthy exercise is almost as important as a change of scenery now and again, And above all else, all members of the Goat clan should look to build a secure base, because it is from here that they choose to view the world. This is a sign with more endurance than even it probably realises and because of this fact some Goats can be a little too careful and have been known to wrap themselves up in cotton wool.

1908
1920
1932
1944
1956
1968
1980
1992
2004

The
Monkey

ABOUT THE MONKEY

Although a diverse group worldwide, nobody would doubt either the success or the intelligence of Monkeys generally. As a species they are adaptable, resourceful, sociable and capable of much deceit. Undoubtedly the Chinese astrologers of old were familiar with this endearing little creature, its winning ways and its mischievous provocations alike, so they were especially astute in naming this department of the zodiac zoo after the Monkey.

Like their animal counterparts, Monkey people like to be on the go as much as any other sign. But it isn't necessary for the Monkey to overdo things. It's true that they are active as a rule, though can take long periods of rest when the sun shines, or if life is particularly dull. What singles this sign out more than anything however is its versatility, for the Monkey can turn his or her hand to almost any task, seemingly with equal and consumate ease. This aspect of the Monkey can upset less capable souls, who often see the type as being show-offs and know-it-alls. The accusation may be a little unfair, since these people genuinely are jacks-of-all-trades, even if as a breed they do tend to lord it over others a little.

The Monkey is keen on fashion, loves to look smart on all occasions and can make the most of any social situation. Getting to the top of the tree is not hard for this particular primate, for there is a good business acumen and an ambition that is likely to match.

Both male and female Monkeys tend to have more than the average amount of sex-appeal, which is one of the reasons why they are often sought out as life-partners by so many other animal signs. Life with this person is usually quite interesting and lives up to the expectations of a wide range of other Chinese signs.

Beware though, for you are not dealing with an easy-touch here. Almost any Monkey can also be very touchy and does not care at all for criticism, which it always takes personally. The Monkey has a very good memory, does not make a good enemy and can be genuinely spiteful at times. Most important of all, the Monkey possesses an ego many times its size and will not be convinced that it has many faults. Most of all it loves to be told how wonderful it is.

THE MONKEY GOOD AND BAD

"That person is too clever by half". This is an exclamation that must have been levelled at the Monkey more than any other species in the human menagerie. The most infuriating fact being that the statement is often true. You can't really class being intelligent, resilient or versatile as constituting faults, and yet in the dexterous hands of the Monkey they can all seem to be just that.

Whatever you say, the Monkey knows better; whatever you are capable of, this capricious little character can do the same thing twice as efficiently and in half the time. In Far Eastern circles the Monkey was often considered to be the king amongst all animals, and observing the Monkey person at work, you might be forgiven for believing that this is still the case.

Nevertheless, this human animal, in some ways, is the most human of all, because it is far more willing than many to show its own vulnerability and its very real insecurity. At best, which is often, the Monkey is as good a working ally as you could ever want to meet, and is very brave, almost to the point of being foolhardy. It can work long and hard for extended periods without a break and will usually champion the underdog, even on those occasions when the dog at the bottom doesn't really want to be championed at all!

In any situation that needs to be considered carefully and with a knowing ability to set matters straight in an instant, the Monkey is the person who you should be looking for. There can be pent-up aggression for bad or good here, so that though the Monkey has been known to start wars, its courage and tenacity can win them too.

More like the proverbial elephant in some respects, this cheeky little creature never forgets, but this doesn't merely extend to those occasions when the Monkey considers itself to have been wronged.

Friendship is usually for life with the Monkey, and on those occasions when you find yourself in trouble, your primate pal will be on-hand to take as much of the load from your shoulders as is humanly possible. Sorting out your problems is as easy as falling off a log for the Monkey, who relishes a challenge and can be more or less guaranteed to rise to any challenge that might happen along.

THE WORKING MONKEY

There is no doubting the fact that the Monkey thinks of him or herself as being a natural leader, which is why this Chinese animal does not take kindly to playing second-fiddle to anyone at all.

The Monkey wants to think up the ideas and then be in a position to put them into practice. Even partial power may not be enough for this person, whose brothers and sisters have composed a fair cross-section of the world's dictators in the past.

Despite this the Monkey is a versatile creature, so you could find it involved in almost any kind of employment, only provided that there is a degree of authority and much personal satisfaction to be had from it. Any job that requires a combination of dexterity and a good memory might suit the primate down to the ground, even though this is the place that you would least expect to find any Monkey, animal or human. The top of the tree is the natural place, and the Monkey may well choose 'small' in terms of self-employment, rather than 'big' in a multi-national company if this is what it takes to be at the head of decision making.

The Monkey makes a good and accommodating employer, as long as things are going the way that it wishes, though it will not tolerate a lazy attitude. This animal type will never ask anyone to do anything that it has not undertaken at some time during its life and is willing to take on menial tasks if necessary, no matter how elevated its own position might be.

The Monkey is approachable at work, as anywhere else, mostly by means of flattery. Ask this creature for its help "because I know that you are better at this than anyone else," and you are almost certain to get all the assistance that you need almost at once.

Your Monkey colleague finds plenty to smile about in life and should keep you happy too, since this is not a difficult person to work with. However, since the Monkey's nature is 'mirror-like', your own spontaneous smiles are important too. Monkeys work at their best when surrounded by happy smiling faces because under such circumstances they find it impossible to avoid wearing a grin themselves that spreads from ear to ear.

LIFE WITH THE MONKEY

Not an ideal partner for everyone, the Monkey is nevertheless interesting to have around, always makes things happen and is generally cheerful (as long as you allow him or her to be in charge). No matter what your relationship with the Monkey may be you can expect intellectual stimulation to be part of the deal.

The Primate is a thinker, so much so that actually getting things done could take a little time. Monkeys make good sexual partners because both male and female can be cheekily provocative, even in an established relationship. Doing all that they can to keep the fires of passion burning, this creature is not a cold-fish at all and positively glows in the warmth of adoration. Write a romantic poem for your Monkey lover and he or she will do almost anything for you, but provoke or upset them, and watch the dust as they disappear up the nearest mental tree.

Monkeys generally want to keep a tidy and comfortable abode, are amenable to travel and enjoy recreation and sport outside of the home. They are lovers of the sunshine and would enjoy the comfort of a beautiful and secluded garden, where in moments of leisure it would be possible for them to simply laze an hour or two away. All the same, this is a contradictory character, because after toasting in the sun for several hours, the Monkey can easily party all night, enjoying the cut and thrust of social interaction.

Although capable of promiscuity in early life, partly owing to an over-active imagination, the Monkey is loyal and doesn't usually stray far from an established relationship. Your Monkey will be happy to stick up for you in almost any situation, though will be certain to tell you later that you should have had more sense than to get into a row.

This is a naturally brave person, retentive, thoughtful and persevering. What it can't manage to achieve in one way, it will approach in another. Not everyone can understand what makes the rather complicated Monkey tick, and there are plenty of people around who don't want to take the trouble. If you are one who does, beware of the processes of thought here though, because there are times when the Monkey cannot avoid being deceptive!

MONKEY COMPATIBILITY

Take a look at the table below to see how the Sign of the Monkey fares in general relationships with other inhabitants of the Chinese Cosmic Zoo. The Maximum score for perfect harmony is 8.

MONKEY + RAT	*= 8*	*MONKEY + OX*	*= 4*
MONKEY + TIGER	*= 1*	*MONKEY + RABBIT*	*= 5*
MONKEY + DRAGON	*= 8*	*MONKEY + SNAKE*	*= 3*
MONKEY + HORSE	*= 4*	*MONKEY + GOAT*	*= 4*
MONKEY + MONKEY	*= 7*	*MONKEY + ROOSTER*	*= 4*
MONKEY + DOG	*= 6*	*MONKEY + PIG*	*= 6*

THE MONKEY AND HEALTH

Most of the time the Monkey is too busy and too interested in life to show much in the way of ill-health, and it seems to be the case that this creature is, on the whole, one of the healthiest animals in the Chinese menagerie.

The Monkey sometimes expects rather more of itself than it is able to give, which in itself could lead to a breakdown in health. Look towards the circulatory system and blood disorders as probably the weakest part of the Monkey constitution. The heart should be protected in later life and a nutritious diet is a successful adjunct to good health.

As with his or her animal counterpart, the Monkey is an omnivore, deriving its food intake from a number of different sources, though bearing in mind the need to keep the blood pure, rich and fatty foods should form only a small part of the diet.

Monkeys can be nervy, even those who do not show the trait outwardly; and they can burn up tremendous amounts of energy very quickly, another fact to be considered when assessing dietary intake. What this creature should never do is to run around at break-neck speed, subsisting on a diet of chocolate bars and biscuits, neither of which do the Monkey much good. Sufficient rest and relaxation is often conspicuous in its absence and the cleverest Monkeys do all they can to ensure that they take a break now and again.

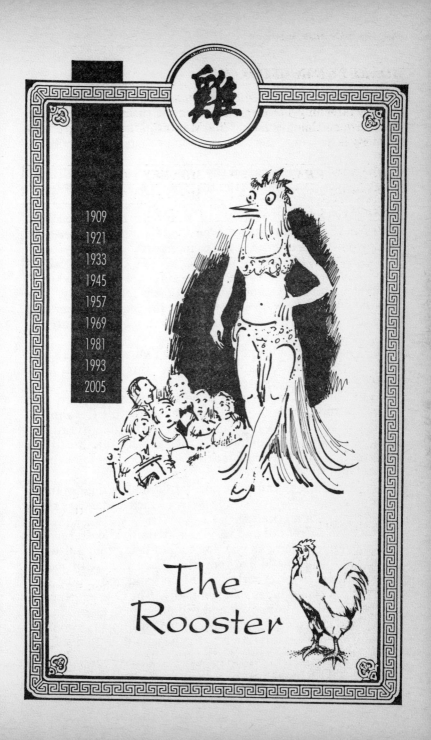

1909
1921
1933
1945
1957
1969
1981
1993
2005

The Rooster

ABOUT THE ROOSTER

A fastidious creature is the Rooster. It's his job to make certain that the hen-run is kept in order and that all his wives are protected. Fussing, clucking and strutting, he keeps up a constant guard, always alert and wanting things exactly his own way.

The similarities between the real-life creatures that must have occupied a central part in the lives of the ancient Chinese, and the characters of the people that they represent, never fail to amaze with their breathtaking accuracy. This is especially true with the human rooster, who shows an uncanny series of similarities to his or her animal counterpart.

This person-Rooster is as stylish as any Cockerel, can be very fussy and fastidious and is certainly not lacking when it comes to expressing a point of view that is felt strongly. The Rooster is keen to put on a show, needs to speak his or her own mind, no matter what anyone else may think to the contrary, and can be very brave when necessary.

Roosters are complex people, and their minds work in a way that may puzzle less complicated types. But you can at least expect them to be fairly consistent.

Basic belief patterns seem to be maintained through long periods of time, often for life. Like that strutting Cock in the farmyard, the human Rooster is inclined to take life rather more seriously than it should, which is why this breed are sometimes accused of being lacking when it comes to having a sense of humour.

Roosters have a natural curiosity that makes them want to know how absolutely everything works, which also makes them splendid jacks of all trades.

Practical, successful and very consistent, the Rooster makes a good friend, as long as you don't mind being told quite frequently how you should live your life. When you are in need of support the Rooster is certain to be on hand and can be very good when it comes to tea and sympathy. The Rooster genuinely does care about humanity and will often go to great lengths to help and assist, even people who it may not know personally. Probably even more importantly, the Rooster is certainly one of the most reliable and trustworthy creatures to be found in the Chinese zodiac.

THE ROOSTER GOOD AND BAD

Perhaps you don't like to be told how you should look, who would best clean your chimney, which person you can afford to trust etc. If this is the case then you will want to steer well clear of the Rooster. He or she really doesn't mean to interfere, they simply cannot help themselves. Because of this they are called busybodies, knowalls and fusspots. All true for the very worst of the brood, but rather unjust when considering the motives behind much of this behaviour.

What could appear to be rank selfishness is quite often a genuine desire, often a burning need, to be of assistance. The Rooster knows its own faults and can be inclined, through some peculiar reverse logic, to put on a more glorious show than ever, in order to compensate.

The tidy-minded Rooster cannot stand any sort of mess, mental or physical. The houses of these people are as clean as a new pin and if you see one, moving this, altering that and straightening the other, the person bears so much of a similarity to the farmyard animal that you could well burst out laughing. When the giggles have died down however, this constant habit of sorting things out could be very annoying, especially if it is your farmyard that comes in for the treatment. The Rooster at his or her worst has got to be the most infuriating person imaginable.

Much of this behaviour is due to a natural nervousness that the Rooster finds impossible to control. When settled and not agitated by life, the other side of the nature begins to show and you find yourself confronted by a reliable ally, a staunch and loyal friend and a very capable mind. The Rooster can deal with a conundrum in a flash and will have any practical task sorted whilst the rest of humanity are still thinking about it. It is Roosters who get down to the practicalities of feeding the Third World and who actually stand between warring factions.

People born under this sign of the Chinese Zodiac almost always display a noteworthy reverence for nature. Most Roosters enjoy being out in the fresh air, are naturally inclined to rolling, pastoral countryside and revel in a life that is free from some of the pressures that towns and cities are inclined to bestow. This is a friendly sign and needs to be popular with those it takes to.

THE WORKING ROOSTER

The Rooster can get through an amazing amount of work, though is not inclined to do so at any great speed. Here we find fast mental processes inside a body that simply refuses to rush, which can cause a little frustration on occasions.

It follows from the character of this fastidious bird that the Rooster would not be happy to take on board any especially dirty or unsavoury job full time, even though the sign is inherently good at sorting out the sort of mess that the rest of us make all the time.

The Rooster likes to be in charge, at least of its own little operation. This may not be interpreted as a quality of leadership, since the Rooster also makes a good employee and a capable second-in-command.

What is vital inside a working situation is that the Rooster is told right from the start exactly what will be expected, how to go about the job and what the end product should be. Once the wise old bird has sorted things out and organised a routine that is suitable, it can carry on doing the same old thing until judgement day if necessary. Here we find a contradiction though, because Roosters welcome and rise to a challenge of any sort, and can become stodgy when faced with repetitive tasks, no matter how good they may be at actually doing them.

If you are looking for an extremely good secretary, mathematician, accountant or office supervisor, don't be surprised if the applicant you prefer turns out to have come straight from the hen-run. Roosters have enough initiative to undertake almost any task, though they may not be especially good in a position that means frequent changes in direction of approach or adapting quickly to changing circumstances. These contradict some of the Roosters basic tendencies.

The Rooster is a thinker, though along logical lines. The imagination is surprisingly good, and Roosters can write well. It is not surprising therefore to discover that many novelists have this sign as a part of their astrological make-up.

If you are busy, and are looking for someone to keep things tidy at home, look after the children and to run things with a combination of Sweet Charity and a camp-commandant, a Rooster house-keeper, male of female could certainly be the answer.

LIFE WITH THE ROOSTER

Roosters can make either the very best partners in life, or the worst, for as with all situation of one-to-one relationships, it also depends on your personality type and needs. If you are a freedom-loving individual, with an insatiable desire to seek out fresh fields and pastures new continually, you could find a Rooster partner far too stifling to meet your needs. But of course there are other things in life that you may consider to be more important than a sense of personal freedom.

Roosters, male and female alike, tend to make very good cooks, always keep a tidy and economical home and can be the most warm-hearted people in the world.

The Rooster really wants to make his or her partner, friend or flat-mate, as happy as possible, for it has been suggested that despite the apparent stability and even stubborness of the sign, caring for and worrying about others is the Roosters main objective in life.

This is a person who you really need to know well. Once you do, as most people in the same shoes would have to agree, you learn to love the Rooster 'warts and all'. Where the more physical aspects of personal relationships are concerned, you should remember that inside that somewhat case-hardened exterior beats a heart of gold and a passion fuelled by the best imagination in the whole menagerie.

Somewhere along the line the suppressed emotion also inherent in the sign has to find an outlet, which in the case of the Rooster is often expressed in the intimacy to be found behind the bedroom door.

As a parent the Rooster is inclined to fuss, cluck and strut about as much as any broody hen, but remember that the underrated farmyard fowl is one of the best parents and guardians in the world, and the human Rooster is not far behind in terms of caring for its brood.

The Rooster in your life may nag, insist, bully and argue, but he or she will try to care for your every need and will probably love you for life. In a world full of shifting values and one in which the basis of relationships can seem to be a complete mystery to many people, the steadfast qualities of the Rooster might be very welcome. Could you really ask for anything more?

ROOSTER COMPATIBILITY

Take a look at the table below to see how the Sign of the Rooster fares in general relationships with other inhabitants of the Chinese Cosmic Zoo. The Maximum score for perfect harmony is 8.

ROOSTER + RAT	= 5	*ROOSTER + OX*	= 8
ROOSTER + TIGER	= 5	*ROOSTER + RABBIT*	= 1
ROOSTER + DRAGON	= 7	*ROOSTER + SNAKE*	= 8
ROOSTER + HORSE	= 5	*ROOSTER + GOAT*	= 4
ROOSTER + MONKEY	= 4	*ROOSTER + ROOSTER*	= 3
ROOSTER + DOG	= 4	*ROOSTER + PIG*	= 4

THE ROOSTER AND HEALTH

At heart the Rooster is a born worrier, in fact it wouldn't be going too far to suggest that the only thing that really upsets the Rooster is not having anything to worry about. This in itself is part of the basic nature of the person and is usually something that they learn to come to terms with, though it can take a toll on the general health ultimately.

It is not unusual to find Roosters who suffer from asthma, and other disorders that can have a partly nervous-based origin. These individuals can also make archetypal hypochondriacs, though are generally much tougher than they give themselves credit for being.

In terms of diet, as with the Monkey, the Rooster is an omnivore. Roosters are often big eaters, so they may have to watch out for weight problems later in life, though the mental motivation often keeps them as thin as a rake.

If you are the Rooster reading this section with special interest, the best advice that could be offered is to live your life with as little stress as possible. Of course stress is often self-induces, especially in your case. However, if you bear this in mind, your health may well take care of itself. Roosters are fairly tough old birds at heart and can tolerate significant physical hardship if necessary.

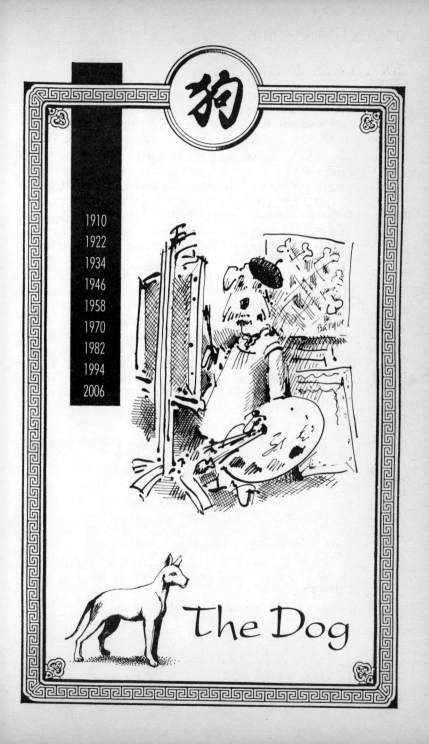

狗

1910
1922
1934
1946
1958
1970
1982
1994
2006

The Dog

ABOUT THE DOG

Once again those observant Chinese scribes of old can be congratulated, not just on account of their knowledge of astrology, but also for their meticulous observance of the world around them; for the good old domestic Dog bears many striking similarities to those people who are affected by the sign named after it.

Probably the most significant likeness lies in the naturally protective quality of the sign, for Dogs are people who want to put a caring arm around anyone who they take to. They can be very brave when it comes to defending the individuals who they see as being their responsibility, which in the case of some Dogs at least is all of humanity.

Dog people are certainly not backward when it comes to having their say. This is a communicative sign that demands to be listened to, and one that could become rather excitable and nervy on those occasions when it is ignored.

As with many signs, there is a slight contradiction relating to the Dog, because this is the sort of person who is also given to short but intense periods of solitude and silence. Usually this would come about as a result of the Dog finding itself amongst people or situations inclined to upset its natural sense of balance. However, the Hound is not a sulker by nature and can always be expected to be on top form quite quickly.

Dog people are fun to have around, and though given to being pessimistic when things are going wrong, it doesn't take much effort to make them light-hearted again. The secret lies in the fact that to the dog, no mood lasts, though this can make it difficult on occasions to know exactly where you stand with this somewhat mercurial character.

The Dog is demure, can charm the skin off a rice-pudding and needs to feel wanted. The nervous system is not especially strong, so the Dog tends to worry about things too much, requiring much encouragement and support from loved ones if it is to give of its best.

The honesty of this person is rarely in doubt, though many Dogs hold radical views and are rarely to be considered conventional. Fully understanding what it is that makes this person tick is never going to be easy, particularly since the Dog him or herself probably is not all that certain either.

THE DOG GOOD AND BAD

Chief amongst the difficult aspects associated with this rather charming person is the apparent inability to make a decision and stick to it. Although this is a criticism often levelled at the Dog, it could be rather unfair, since the truth of the matter is that the Dog really does want to bear everyone in mind before it makes up its mind about anything. Most people realise that to do so is only possible up to a point, though this is a consideration that only serves to complicate life even more for the Canine counterpart. Leave the Dog alone however and it will eventually make a sensible and rational choice.

The Dog is given to being rather spendthrift on occasions, and although you could quite easily set the Hound to guard the Bank of England with absolute trust, when it comes to his or her own resources, the Dog is not quite so careful. This can make for an somewhat precarious financial situation in the Dog household, though on the positive side, the Mut is a good worker and can be guaranteed to get itself out of any mess that it recognises as being self-created.

Dogs are real charmers, which although usually considered a virtue, could also be a vice in certain circumstances. Partly because the Dog is so naturally affectionate, and a little insecure, it is also apt to wander in terms of relationships. The Dog is therefore not to be considered the most steadfast animal in the menagerie when it comes to emotional ties. Despite this, the Dog is capable of proving itself very loyal, is brave to the point of being foolhardy, loves to please everyone and wants to make a favourable impression wherever it goes.

Give a dog a bad name and it's certain to stick. Yet there are a world of people who are willing to rely absolutely on their canine cronies. This may not be the most easily understood animal in the zoo, though it is one of the most likeable. All Dogs love to wag their tails after all and the one who you find yourelf attached to in one way or another is not likely to be an exception to this rule. Remember too however, that if cornered or under threat, Dogs are tenacious fighters. In the case of the Chinese Dog type this tendency would usually be considered amongst the good points, particularly where the defence of loved ones is concerned, though this is not to infer that the Dog is incapable of selfish actions too on occasions.

THE WORKING DOG

The Dog is naturally cheerful, is capable of working long and hard, as long as there is sufficient interest involved in the task, and will be quite happy to work in the company of others. Because this person is so adaptable, you could find them involved in almost any type of employment, though it is true that the Dog does not take especially well to dirty jobs, which may be part of the reason that the sign is often drawn towards clerical work of one sort or another.

In the field of personnel work the Dog excels, likewise with counselling of any sort, for here we have a person who is capable of talking well enough, but one that makes a good listener too. The Dog is quite able to sort out the problems of the world, though less good at dealing with its own. For this reason it is important for the Hound to get its own house in order if it is to work at anything in a disciplined and ordered way.

Some people accuse the Dog of being inconsistent, though this would probably only be the case for those carrying the sign by year, Moon and Ascendant. More commonly there are other, more fixed, elements to the nature that allow the endearing qualities of the Dog to predominate, though without the lack of consistency found in the archetype.

Dogs make good bankers, accountants and auditors, because once committed they are capable of working with great care. Usually there is a creative side to the sign too, so that many of the worlds great artists have carried qualities of this sign in their own natures. Dog's are found amongst designers, graphic artists and teachers of art. In most professions they are fun to be with, love the cut and thrust of working life, but like to know what is expected of them.

This is a sign that loves to travel and revels in languages. Not surprising therefore, bearing in mind the other attributes of the type, that many of the world's greatest diplomats have been born when the Dog predominated. The Dog combines the ability to jump on and off aeroplanes, buses and trains with an ability to slot into just about any sort of culture. This sign has great respect for the customs of those it comes into contact with and can usually be relied upon to bring only praise upon itself, its company and its nation when travelling abroad.

LIFE WITH THE DOG

Many people would happily choose a Dog for a soul-mate or a friend, over and above any other Chinese sign. The reason is obvious; the sign is so affable by nature that it is very difficult to fall out with. True, the Dog can be quite excitable and even a little outspoken at times, though it is rarely, if ever, malicious, is not known to be especially moody and will usually fall in line with the ideas of those with whom it lives.

Dog people do not set out to rule the household and will generally be happy to live an uncomplicated life, if it only proves possible to do so. Here we could have the fly in the ointment, because there is no doubt that the Dog does tend to lead a disjointed existence, even though this does not appear to be a situation that it actively chooses. It is within this complicated web of activity, intrigue and confusion that you may find yourself projected, should you decide that life with the Dog is for you.

The only other real problem sometimes encountered in this scenario stems from the Dog's inability to remain faithful in thought, word and deed. As long as this member of the zoo is happy and interested in a full social and personal life, all is well. The worst of all cases only occurs when the Dog is unhappy, or perhaps feels neglected. Under such circumstances the Dog may choose to look around for more stimulating company, beyond which it is all too easy for one unfortunate thing to lead to another.

Those living with a Dog individual and involved with one personally, would do well to remember that variety is the spice of life to this critter. When this fact is understood and catered for, you will not meet a better person in the whole breadth and length of the menagerie.

Dogs look after their families well, are protective spouses and can be tremendously encouraging to less motivated types. They are as anxious to see you succeed in life as they are to get on themselves, and as a result can be very supportive. Romantically speaking, they never tire of hearts and roses and usually can be relied upon to keep their lovers supplied with compliments at all times. The reality of living with the Dog might be slightly different however, for Dog people are subject to mood swings that require some gentle coaxing.

DOG COMPATIBILITY

Take a look at the table below to see how the Sign of the Dog fares in general relationships with other inhabitants of the Chinese Cosmic Zoo. The Maximum score for perfect harmony is 8.

DOG + RAT	*= 6*	*DOG + OX*	*= 3*
DOG + TIGER	*= 8*	*DOG + RABBIT*	*= 7*
DOG + DRAGON	*= 1*	*DOG + SNAKE*	*= 6*
DOG + HORSE	*= 8*	*DOG + GOAT*	*= 3*
DOG + MONKEY	*= 6*	*DOG + ROOSTER*	*= 4*
DOG + DOG	*= 6*	*DOG + PIG*	*= 6*

THE DOG AND HEALTH

Although not the most robust of the human animals to be found in the Chinese menagerie, the Dog can do more to help itself than most other signs.

The motivating principle is the nervous system, and the main physical points of reference are the throat and the kidneys. Failure to observe a reasonably sensible routine and a healthy diet could easily lead to problems in these areas of the anatomy. However, much of the nervous activity stimulated by the Dog is apt to find its way to the surface via the outspoken and excitable nature of this sign, a much better state of affairs than the repressive tendencies shown by some other zodiac signs.

Happiness is important of course, probably more so than any other consideration, for the Dog is surprisingly resilient and can even tolerate material deprivation, as long as personal contentment is not absent. Remove stimulating company and the Dog may become lethargic, melancholic and eventually ill. Dog people need plenty of fresh air and good healthy walks in the country if they are to remain as healthy as they should be, and they should never work themselves to the point of exhaustion in their desire to achieve everything all at once.

Comfort and security may be the best assurance of good health, together with a knowledge that they are surrounded by love.

豬

1911
1923
1935
1947
1959
1971
1983
1995
2007

The Pig

ABOUT THE PIG

The Pig has gained itself a rather problematic reputation, the more so in its domestic state. However, this is a very different creature from the animal that the ancient Chinese were familiar with, and it is within the realms of the present day Pig's wilder ancestors that we find the best similarities with the zodiac Pig person.

Pigs are basically shy creatures in the wild, they have to be, because they are vulnerable to attack and make a tasty snack for any would be predator. Not that they are defenceless, as many an unwary hunter discovered to his cost, for although often willing to stay in the undergrowth, all Pigs, animal and human, can fight ferociously if they have to do so, and in the case of the human variety at least, rarely lose a battle once they are committed.

This is probably the most underestimated of all the Chinese signs, and also one of the most difficult to understand. The Pig is full of apparent paradoxes, it is shy and demure, though powerful and tenacious; it may hide in a corner when unexpected company is about, and yet is primed to act quickly and with frightening certainty when it proves necessary to do so.

Pigs are usually kind by disposition, though do have the reputation for being a little dark and mysterious. They are highly charged sensually and can love to the point of excluding all other considerations from their minds. They relish being at home and want to make the most of family life, in which they find the greatest happiness of all.

Pigs work hard, both on their own account and for any enterprise or charity that they really believe in. Many people think that they can detect a certain vulnerability, or even a gullible streak, in the Pigs basic nature. This may be true, but exploit it at your own peril. If you think in terms of some over-fed porker, lounging lazily in a sty and waiting for the butcher to arrive, then think again. The Pig type is intelligent, can struggle long and hard in order to achieve its objectives, responds well to love and attention and is, in every way, a unique individual. Looks, not to mention first impressions, can be very deceptive, and especially so in this case. The Pig is probably the kindest, though potentially the most dangerous animal in the whole menagerie.

THE PIG GOOD AND BAD

Pig-people are kind, sociable and very loyal, so it may not be easy on first impressions to see anything below the surface that would look at all threatening or sinister. Pigs can work long and hard for others, take a great delight in being of assistance and will go to almost any lengths to please a friend. However, it might be suggested that they do all these things entirely on their own terms, because they are equally capable of being conniving, scheming, and even malicious if they are crossed or upset. This is what makes the Pig such a difficult sign to deal with, and could be part of the reason why it is not as popular as perhaps it should be.

Pigs are not usually radical in their approach to life, appearing to be quite able to take the line of least resistance. They are very hard-working and can stick to the task in hand as well as any of their animal cousins. What sets them apart however, is a fixed quality that has no equal elsewhere in the zoo. If the Pig decides it is going to take a certain course of action, no matter how foolhardy or ill-advised it may obviously be, there is nothing that can be done to divert it. Pig-people often come from rather difficult family backgrounds, and this may be part of the reason why Pigs are usually so determined to ensure that nothing will interfere with their own family, which is usually of singular importance to the sign.

The mystery that surrounds people born under this sign, can be both a blessing and a curse on occasions. In relationships there is liable to be a mystique that is truly magnetic and lasting, though if you are merely an acquaintance the Pig may seriously insult you with its closed attitudes. Such dense curtains of mystery can surround some Pigs, that the observer may think it not worth the effort to penetrate them. Even the most outgoing, life-loving Pig in the sty is capable of putting up shields that would be impenetrable to all but the most perceptive individual.

Pigs are all sensualists at heart and love to indulge their love of luxury. Most of the time this is a harmless enough facet of the porker's nature. Though there are times when the rest of the world may find the Pigs obsessions for bathing, eating, sleeping and the rest to be just a little tiresome. If you live with a Pig, you may have installed a second bathroom already!

THE WORKING PIG

Although Pigs can be good and tireless workers, they also know how to enjoy the finer things in life and can be great sensualists. They are reasonably adaptable and like a little variety in their lives if at all possible. This is not to suggest that a Pig would refuse repetitive employment however, for there is something about continuity that appeals to the Piggy nature. The only problem when repetition forms part of the working scenario is that the job in hand may not utilise the Pig's very good mind fully enough, which could lead to a somewhat mischievous worker in the fullness of time.

Since Pigs are not squeamish by nature, sometimes even taking a certain delight in the sort of situation that would have more sensitive types reeling in horror, Pigs make excellent doctors and nurses. This role would also fulfil the Pig-person's need to be of use to humanity. Veterinary surgeons also often have Pig contacts in their makeup because this sign is especially fond of animals.

All Pigs are ready to face up to a challenge and can be very brave when confronted by adversity. This sign favours the armed-forces, or any job that offers a physical dimension. In fact this may appear to be something of a paradox because the Pig definitely does have a lazy streak and some unkind souls have suggested that the Pig loves to tire itself out merely so that it can spend the next couple of days in bed! The occasional reserved period can make it difficult for co-workers to know exactly how the Pig is thinking, day to day, no matter what occupation may be chosen.

This is not a sign that takes very well to being told what to do, unless the person doing the telling is capable of being diplomatic. Pigs are not plodders however, and can make a singular success of their business lives.

The Pig is an ideal candidate for self-employment because the sign is capable of much self-motivation and can make a good and reasonable employer. In this, as with other aspects of work, it is worth remembering that the Pig either gets on extremely well with the people in its vicinity, or dislikes them intensely. To this animal there are very few shades of grey. However, being adaptable, Pigs occupy many walks of life, and usually with significant success.

LIFE WITH THE PIG

The sign of the Pig has got to be either the easiest of the Chinese zodiac types to live with, or the hardest; it really depends on the type of relationship and the nature of the person opposite.

The Pig is looking for a settled sort of existence, loving to put its trotters up in front of the fire where it basks in the adoration of a loving family. One major problem arises from the fact that here we have a person to whom getting their own way is about as important as breathing. Once again we stumble across an astrological paradox, because for most of the time the Pig is an easy-going type and is often quite willing to defer to the choices made by others. It is only when the Pig is faced with a request that sounds more like an order that problems arise, for when this person digs in their heels and refuses to move, you may as well quit, because the Pig never will. The secret is to use a little psychology, to make many tentative suggestions and few actual statements. As long as the Pig believes that he or she is making the running, you should be able to have things pretty-much your own way.

Your Pig lover will do everything within his or her power to make you happy. The Pig is generous and kind, extremely sensual and definitely geared to a highly-charged physical relationship.

When it comes to getting jobs done around the house, Pigs are usually creative and practical. The way that the Pig's home appears to others is quite important, and so much time and energy will be spent getting everything looking just as it should.

When young, the Pig can boogy with the best of them, and is often to be found down at the disco, looking smart and appealing and willing to dance the night away. As time passes, so the Pig tends to become a little sedentary, more content to stay close to the home, and many Pigs also become rather over-fixed in their attitudes. Pig-people generally love children and can make splendid parents, even if on occasion they do tend to be a little over-cautious and inclined to smother their offspring with just a little too much concern. Pig people are often readers and enjoy a good story. This makes them fairly literary by inclination and often above average in intelligence.

PIG COMPATIBILITY

Take a look at the table below to see how the Sign of the Pig fares in general relationships with other inhabitants of the Chinese Cosmic Zoo. The Maximum score for perfect harmony is 8.

PIG + RAT	= 6	**PIG + OX**	= 5
PIG + TIGER	= 7	**PIG + RABBIT**	= 8
PIG + DRAGON	= 6	**PIG + SNAKE**	= 1
PIG + HORSE	= 6	**PIG + GOAT**	= 8
PIG + MONKEY	= 6	**PIG + ROOSTER**	= 4
PIG + DOG	= 6	**PIG + PIG**	= 6

THE PIG AND HEALTH

The Pig type is generally fairly healthy, though as is the case with many signs, much depends on the Pig's state of mind in addition to the sort of life that it may be living in a strictly day-to-day sense. It's true that Pig individuals can be a little too self-indulgent for their own good on occasions and this could lead to some obesity, especially in middle years.

Parts of the body said to be significant in the case of the Pig include the reproductive organs and the stomach. To stay at the peak of physical fitness Pig types need to look to regular exercise, plenty of good, healthy food and a fairly ordered routine. Those born under the sign of the Pig are inclined to drink more than is sometimes strictly good for them and need to be careful to avoid excesses of all kinds.

The average Pig individual is probably more robust than most and can deal relatively easily with adversity, particularly when there is a good cause, ie. showing concern for others and particularly members of the family. This individual will quite happily go without in a personal sense in order to make life more comfortable for those people who are most important. Repression of feelings is a danger to the Pig, who responds to a truthful approach to all situations. However, the Pig sometimes finds it difficult to express itself and this can lead to internalised frustration, which in itself can be a slight danger in terms of lasting good health.

CHINESE ELEMENTS AND WHAT THEY MEAN

In the introduction to this book on Chinese astrology, you will recall that mention was made of a 60-year cycle favoured by the Chinese astrologers of old. This is a significant factor uniting Eastern and Western traditions in astrology, because it exists in both systems. Not only is 60 years a third of the 'Great Solar Round' of 180 years (at the end of which the planets tend to group on the same side of the Sun) but it is also the first time that the number of orbits of the solar system's giants Jupiter and Saturn are subdivisible (5 orbits of Jupiter = roughly 60 years. 2 orbits of Saturn = roughly 60 years).

The planetary relevance of the 60-year cycle to the Chinese, who certainly knew just as much about the solar system as the Babylonians or Egyptians, seems to have been forgotten or obscured in their fascination with the Sun and Moon. However, it is retained in their assigning every animal year to one of 5 elements. Thus when all 12 signs had been through all five elements (5 x 12), a period of 60 years would have elapsed.

"What has all this got to do with me?" I hear you ask. And the answer is that a knowledge of the elements and which ones have a bearing on you is fundamental to really understanding just what astute observers of the heavens (and of humanity) the Chinese scribes really were. You will find what Element ruled the year of your birth by referring to the tables on pages 4 and 5 where it is listed together with the Animal that ruled the year of your birth.

On the pages that follow this section, you will find a description of each Animal Sign and the way it is altered by every Element. A look at your own combination will show how you differ from the more routine aspects of your ruling Animal Sign and you can learn which aspects of nature are specific to your Element and Animal combined. The five Elements are Metal, Water, Wood, Fire and Earth. There is some correspondence here with the more familiar Elements used in Western Astrology, which, as in so many other aspects of the craft, seems to indicate that the origins of astrological study lies so far back in the mists of time that each branch must originally have had a common ancestor. However, the Chinese eventually opted for a five Element system, and so took a path not followed by any other major culture.

THE CHINESE ELEMENTS

METAL

Metal makes for a rigid nature, that does not give in easily and insists on extra effort, both from itself and from other people with whom its possessor comes into contact. There is great strength of character here.

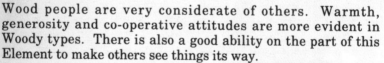

WATER

Water people are usually thought of as being very creative. There is a compassion and an understanding here that reduces the more caustic qualities of any sign, allowing kindness to shine out more prominently.

WOOD

Wood people are very considerate of others. Warmth, generosity and co-operative attitudes are more evident in Woody types. There is also a good ability on the part of this Element to make others see things its way.

FIRE

As the Element itself indicates, Fire makes for a dynamic quality to the nature. Fire people have great strength of purpose and are rarely diverted from any course of action that they see as being of importance.

EARTH

Patience is the greatest virtue that Earth people possess. They can work long and hard to see their ideas come to fruition, and constantly strive to make themselves more successful. This Element can be very stubborn however.

METAL RAT

Since the Rat is already a very dynamic character, there is no doubt that the addition of the Metal Element will do much to increase the positive qualities of the sign, occasionally to the detriment of the kind and forgiving Rat nature.

Metal present makes for greater bite to the nature and bestows a keener sense of urgency. It allows for a more passionate tendency, also tending to eradicate some of the potentially weaker traits. It might be argued that the basic Rat nature is actually altered very little by the presence of Metal here. After all, you can do little to improve on perfection, and in the mind of the Metal Rat itself at least, the subconscious presence of this Element will only serve to confirm that he or she is really a 'pretty together sort of person'. Unfortunately this may not be the opinion of the world at large, for although the Metal Rat may be bounding with energy, overflowing with self-confidence and full to the brim with passion, does it really look out at the world through wiser eyes as a result?

This Rat is basically as concerned and caring as all the rest, though it may be less likely to carry the virtue of understanding, and can easily be accused of chasing self-interest. Despite all this, here we have a Rat who is determined to succeed in life, no matter what obstacles may be laid in its path. Taking the naturally resourceful qualities inherent in the sign, the Metal Rat sharpens them all to perfection. This is an adaptable and unquestionably successful Rat, even though to some it may not appear to be constantly endearing. Beauty is in the eye of the beholder however and there are many individuals who would find much to praise in the dynamic, capable Metal Rat.

WATER

WATER RAT

Keneth Graham, author of *Wind in the Willows* would have recognised this character, for it is so reminiscent of the Water Rat of his creation. Ratty was an extremely capable character, able to deal with the dreaded weasels, who had everyone else so worried. He was courageous and resourceful, but he also understood what made less positive types, such as the timid Mole, tick. Water makes for a more tolerant nature and allows the powers of communication to really come into their own. As a result this Rat makes its best approach to life through understanding and communication.

The Water Rat knows its own limitations better than the rest of the Rat clan, though it does not allow them to get in the way. Utilising diplomacy on those occasions that other Rats might choose to barge in, the Water Rat usually gets what it wants out of life. Confrontation is not always the best way to proceed, and this creature instinctively realises the fact.

Neither is the Water Rat quite so inclined to judge as it's cousins may, though it still retains a healthy temper on occasions. Dear Ratty himself sometimes became rather angry at the ridiculous behaviour of less 'centered' animals such as Mr Toad, yet at the end of his anger he could be relied upon to act with consideration and empathy, even towards the boastful and capricious Toad. So it is to some extent with all Water Rats, who delight in helping out whenever the opportunity to do so arises. They may not carve quite the path for themselves in life that would be the case with Metal or Fire, especially in terms of wealth and prestige, though to compensate, they have a serenity of nature that their brother and sister Rats might well envy. Water Rat is probably the wisest of the rodent family.

WOOD RAT

The Wood Rat is much less likely to be found running the 'used car department' than are other members of the Rat-race. The reason for this is that Wood brings a more ethical quality to the nature and in the case of the Rat, this removes the 'wide boy' feel that sometimes attends the sign in its most exuberant form. The Wood Rat could be an altogether quieter type, willing to stand back and watch the flowers grow and probably better able to settle to a routine sort of existence than would be the case with either Metal or Fire. The natural generosity of the Rat is, if anything, even greater in the presence of a Wood association, so that these individuals can and often do spend a great deal of their time helping others out.

One of the greatest potential problems for the Rat is a natural tendency on occasions to take on more than is really sensible. This can lead to some failures in life and may also result in physical exhaustion. The Wood element makes such situations less likely, removing some of the urgency that follows the Rat through all situations. As a result, this is a calm rodent, still very capable and reasonably successful, but with greater consideration and less in the way of anxiety.

There are a few drawbacks here. For one, the Rat is a naturally speculative person, and this makes for a fair percentage of the interest that Rats generate on their journey through life. Being naturally more careful, the Wood Rat is less likely to stick its neck out. Although this means less chance of going wrong, it also indicates that the Wood Rat has to work for longer to achieve the same results. The Rat generally lacks patience, so there could be a contradiction to resolve here.

FIRE RAT

Here is the Rat in its most outgoing and high-spirited costume. This is the party Rat, the go-getter with a need to achieve and to be seen to achieve. Strength, energy and dynamism are the qualities that Fire bestows, and when you bear in mind that the Rat is already a fairly dynamic creature, the addition of extra'punch', makes for a character who is not easily duped, rarely bettered and always willing to have go.

It takes energy just to watch the Fire Rat in operation and woe-betide any individual who cannot keep up with this Sign-Element combination. Fire Rats are adventurous, make excellent travellers and love to have a challenge in their sights. Work tends to be best when it offers the chance to interact, partly because the Fire Rat loves the cut and thrust that relationships represent but also because the Rat is in any case a 'people person'; in this as in almost everything, the presence of Fire only serves to amplify the qualities already inherent within the sign of the Rat.

Perhaps the greatest gift that Fire offers to any Rat is an ability to better motivate others. The Rodent does like to be helpful, though will often look towards its own interests first and foremost. The Fire Rat has sufficient energy and enterprise to want to feather the nests of others, as well as its own. You could find this character to be a little too self-possessed and even vain. As with all other combinations in Chinese astrology, much is going to depend on the Moon Sign and also on the Rising sign.

The very worst Fire Rat can be overbearing and dominating, whist the best examples are warm, caring and just about as helpful as any person you are likely to meet.

EARTH RAT

The one thing that can be more or less relied on in the case of individuals who have Earth attached to their Chinese sign, is that a greater degree of stability will be inherent in the basic nature. This can be a distinct advantage in the case of the Rat, who does suffer from a dearth of continuity and a natural tendency to take on too many tasks at the same time.

The Earth Rat could be somewhat quieter than other members of the Rat family, and may exhibit a more thoughtful approach to life, especially to new incentives. Nothing of the basic Rat nature is lost, because Earth tends to help rather than hinder the natural positive qualities of 'Rattyness'. Confidence is usually high with this character and there is an ability to look at life more philosophically. Patience is more endemic, something any Rat needs as much of as he or she is able to get their hands on, and the Earth rodent can also usually be found in positions of ultimate responsibility, thanks to a mixture of genuine common sense and an ability to look at life from a detached viewpoint.

In relationships this Rat is quite constant and would seem to offer many of the qualities that a more restricted mind would seek. With less of an urge to dash off at the first chance of a new adventure, the Earth Rat will also be more inclined to settle for less in the way of material pleasures, opting instead to seek out a contented lot in life.

This is a generally happy type, always helpful and anxious to help out its less well off associates and friends. It can be more or less guaranteed to look on the bright side of things. All in all there is every reason to believe that the archetype Earth Rat can be one of the most successful and well-motivated creatures to be found in the menagerie.

METAL OX

The Ox is well known for being something of a stick-in-the-mud, so the presence of Metal here may turn out to be no bad thing. The addition of this Element is certain to increase the natural passion of the cool Ox, turning up the temperature and allowing the Bovine plodder to use some of its patience and determination in a more dynamic way. Of course there are certain to be drawbacks. For example. when the Ox decides that the time has come to dig its heels in about anything, there is nobody around who can shift the lumbering creature. An excess of Metal in the nature could transfix the Ox more than ever, making for probably the most stubborn person imaginable.

Although Ox people are hard workers, and usually achieve much by dint of hard work and perseverance, Metal Ox individuals can be quicker arriving at their objectives. There is terrific self-reliance here, usually allied to a strong physique and a tireless approach to those aspects of life that the Metal Ox sees as being of the greatest interest. In relationships this member of the herd is very passionate, and may possess the ability to speak words of love that the Ox alone would find difficult to mouth. A word of caution however; the Ox is rather inclined to jealousy, and the addition of some Metal in the character could serve to make matters worse, and since it isn't sensible to get on the wrong side of an enraged Ox, it might be best to avoid creating the situation in the first place.

The Metal Ox is a good parent, a loyal and rewarding friend, has much more humour than might be expected from other characters in the Ox family. Above all, here we find dependency alongside action, not a combination that is always to be expected in the Ox enclosure!

WATER OX

There is one area of life that the Ox often finds some difficulty with, namely the sphere of communication. It isn't that the Ox refuses to tell other people how it feels, and there is no doubt that there is much going on behind that often furrowed brow; the problem is actually finding the right words. This is where the Water Element can be of tremendous help and there is no doubt that here we find a good combination of Animal and Element. This is a particularly caring Ox, or at least one who is able to express his or her concern more readily. In addition, Water helps to mitigate some of the more obstinate qualities of the sign, so that as well as being its usual contemplative self, the Water Ox is also willing to compromise; something for which this sign is by no means famous.

New ideas come easily to this member of the Buffalo herd, so that a greater degree of early success in life is to be expected in this case.

The Ox never lacks the ability to think logically, or to work hard, but like a toy car with no reverse gear, the standard Ox is inclined to bump along the wall, rather than changing direction when it would be most advisable to do so. The Water Ox is more likely to look at things in over-view, without the need to make early judgements that would prevent a change of direction at a later date.

Equally important, the inclusion of Water in the nature also inspires the Ox in terms of optional interests, creating the opening for possibilities beyond the scope of a constant 'slog' towards the chosen objective in life. This Ox will still get where it wants to go, and woe-betide anyone who tries to prevent it. The difference here is that it may stop to smell the flowers en-route.

WOOD OX

Some say that here we have the Element most suited to the Ox temperament, and in many ways this would appear to be the case. The Wood Ox is very co-operative, and is inclined to use its tremendous potential for continued effort mainly for the good of others. Wood always brings warmth to the nature, and nowhere is this expressed more subtly, though to greater effect, than in the case of the Ox. Many people fail altogether to see the real emotion that under-pins the nature of most Ox types, though to the Wood Ox this is less of a problem, since this creature displays its feelings far more readily. It isn't that the Wood Ox is any more giving or caring than the rest of the herd, simply that it expresses its concerns and as a result is also able to handle them.

This may not be the loudest member of the Buffalo fraternity, since the Wood serves to make for thoughtfulness, something that the Ox already knows plenty about. A Wood Ox in the family is hardly likely to be told to 'quiten down' very often. There is refinement here in abundance; the Wood Ox always wants to look good, can be relied upon to act with discretion and taste and would not be found lacking in any sort of company. However, this is not a type that copes very well with squalid or even untidy surroundings. Wood Ox people are invariably to be found in 'clean' employment and, as with other members of the herd, they can work long and hard to achieve their objectives in life.

Above all there is great concern for the world as a whole here, which is why the Wood Ox is so often to be found in the sort of situation that serves humanity in one way or another. Serving is the key to personal happiness and also towards a higher degree of personal success.

FIRE OX

Here we have application allied to power, a formidable combination at times and one that could make for the most materially successful member of the Ox family. The real drawback potentially seems to be the fact that so much Fire in the nature could just mean that the Ox manages to burn itself out before it is able to reach its ultimate goals in life. This would not be a particularly good prognosis in terms of general health either.

The Ox is a plodder by nature, and works best when there is nobody prodding it up the rear to gain immediate results. With the Fire Ox, the coaxing comes from within, so that here we find an animal that may on occasions be slightly at odds with itself. The Fire Ox needs to cultivate a quiet and contemplative attitude, saving the dynamism and grit of the hot Element until it is really needed. As long as this balance can be established, there is latent power here to move mountains. Something is always happening in the lives of people who have this combination, which can make them very interesting types to live with, though the worst of the breed could just expect everyone in their vicinity to have exactly the same amount of drive and perseverance that they naturally possess.

There is no lack of compassion when Fire meets the Ox, at least not if the recipient comes to realise that gifts are given to be used for the good of others as well as self. This is a fact that the Ox is usually well aware of, and when it comes to being a driving force for any issue that it feels to be of real importance, the Fire Ox is formidable.

This is definitely a force to be reckoned with, and no Fire Ox should be underestimated by those Chinese signs that may consider themselves to be more dynamic than the careful Ox.

EARTH OX

Look at any herd of wild buffalo and chances are that you will spy one somewhere within the herd that is always the last to arrive, which manages to find more fodder than the rest and which can be guaranteed to conserve energy on all occasions. The human counterpart for this particular animal is the Earth Ox. This is not a person who could be made to do anything that went against the grain. As stubborn as the day is long, this Ox is often disgustingly healthy and always has a pleasant nature.

The Earth Ox will never find itself out in the cold, the reason being that despite its plodding ways, it may turn out to be the best worker of the whole Ox clan. Here we have a natural home-maker and a loving partner. True, the typical Earth Ox is not the most exciting person in the world, but if you are looking for reliability, a generally sunny disposition, above average powers of discrimination and an earthy common sense - this is your man or woman. There is usually enough confidence to back-up the opinions, mainly because the Earth Ox is not inclined to guess in the first place. If an Earth Ox carpenter turns up at your house with a new front door, saying that it will fit, then you can rely on the fact that it will.

What isn't so pleasant about this character is the knowledge that he or she is capable of doing the same thing in an identical manner every day of his or her life, without ever becoming bored. Imagination is not number one on the agenda either, which is why the Earth Ox replicates rather than innovates. Not that this hinders practical skills, for here we have the best engineer, electrician or stone-mason in the whole zoo. If you want something doing around your house, look out for this character.

METAL TIGER

Although the Tiger generally shows a preference to walk alone, especially in terms of emotional attachments, the Metal Tiger can be a slightly different animal. The single-minded aspect of this Element usually works well alongside the rather detached qualities that the sign often displays and this does make for a more passionate pussy-cat. However, it should be remembered that the sign of the Tiger is strong enough to stand alone in almost any situation, and so the addition of any Element is only of quite low importance when judging the overall nature.

Nevertheless we have a Tiger to be reckoned with here. This is, in any case, an animal that desires to have its own way in life, even if it manages to convince you that its requirements are yours too. Add Metal to this scenario and you have a Tiger who really can pull the wool over your eyes, and one who will not hesitate to do so at almost every opportunity. This may not be as problematic as it sounds however, for the Tiger is altruistic and cares deeply about its friends and associates. Metal may bestow greater determination, though it is invariably used to do the 'right thing.'

The Metal Tiger is not quite so reckless as its standard brother or sister may be and although more adventurous, could be inclined to weigh up the pros and cons of any given situation more carefully. Here we have a natural politician, though one who may decide to go his or her own way on the back-benches, rather than sacrificing principle in order to gain power for its own sake. Although still very liberated and as freedom loving as any member of the Tiger clan, the Metal Tiger is a good friend, a trustworthy lover and an enemy you would not wish to make.

WATER TIGER

It isn't at all certain that this combination of Animal and Element does many favours for either, because the two are often at odds with each other. Water implies a compliant and understanding nature, though if this serves to create a Tiger that loses all sense of the 'hunt' in life, it can make for a rather low-key specimen at times and one that can often be unsure of its place in things. All the same, there are compensations. For example, here we have a Tiger who is much more likely to stay at home for more than five minutes at a time. The Water Tiger also finds less difficulty in explaining the twists and turns of its sometimes unusual nature and is more likely than the standard cat to opt for the line of least resistance.

Although some of the genuine mystique of the sign is missing, the Water Tiger turns out to be far more altruistic than any of its cousins carrying other Elements, and you can be certain that this is the best family Tiger of all.

Water does little to alter the reckless nature of the sign, though this brand of Tiger will probably get into less scrapes in the first place. Although a party animal by inclination, the Water Tiger may well choose a corner from which to direct proceedings and can often be found talking things over with people who are troubled in some way, a fact that really does set this cat apart.

Part of the great attraction of Tiger people is their unpredictability, and this is one quality that is certainly put under a degree of restraint when Water is present in the nature. Water Tigers have a warmth that is certain to take some of the 'distance' from the sign. And if you like your cats to roll over for their tummy to be tickled, you could have the right feline here!

WOOD TIGER

There is an aspect to the Tiger that some people find difficult to come to terms with, for despite the Tiger individual being affable enough on the surface, sensitive types are often left with the impression that they never really get to know what makes the Tiger tick. When the Wood Element is present in the nature of a Tiger person, there is more apparent warmth and a better understanding of how to greet the world on a one-to-one basis. This contributes to making for a very popular cat and can also indicate more in the sense of worldly success.

The Wood Tiger is a very generous person, both in terms of time and money. Parents with this combination get on especially well with their children and are often more childlike than their siblings. This Tiger has a great zest for life it's true, though it may be the only member of the family who is inclined to take in slightly more than is good for it in a day-to-day sense. Although the Wood Tiger can often be found quietly ruminating in a corner, this is not as a result of any overtly passive quality within the nature, but can be put down to the fact that this feline is a great thinker as well as an active doer.

When other Tigers are disappearing over the next horizon, in search of fresh fields and pastures new, the Wood Tiger is often to be found at home, for this animal knows that some of the best flights you can book yourself onto are flights of the imagination. The Wood Tiger is a better saver than most of its cousins and can amass significant wealth through patience and hard work. Since there is always a new idea coming along that usually only lacks finance to make it viable, this Tiger could be on the way to making a fortune. And despite the affability, the Wood Tiger still has sharp and dangerous claws.

FIRE TIGER

Here we have the most dynamic inhabitant of the Tiger's enclosure, and one who should not be underestimated at any time. Some say that the sign of the Tiger naturally belongs in this Element, but this would be to underestimate the subtlety of the group as a whole. What Fire does lend to the Tiger is a greater sense of direction in life, more power and a greater potential for the use of force in a day-to-day sense.

With regard to the naturally reckless streak to be found in most Tigers, the Fire present here tends to make matters worse, which is why in business the Fire Tiger could either become a millionaire overnight, or else go out of business as a result of one hasty decision. Still, there is always the option to start again from scratch and to make the most of any opportunity that happens along. The Fire Tiger is astute, well intentioned, usually happy and always willing to help out if it can.

The greatest part that Fire has to play in this nature is to increase the longing for freedom on every level. This is not a person who would want to be tied down to too many routines and one who can be just as happy when alone as when in company. Don't try to work out which way the Fire Tiger will spring, because he or she will fool you every time. There is more than a touch of genius here and a desire to push the frontiers of knowledge further and further along.

Nearly all Fire Tigers are creative in one way or another, which is why they make fine artists and musicians; that is if they stay around long enough to concentrate on such genteel pastimes. Here we have the natural explorer, politician and radical social reformer who will stop at nothing to do what he or she wants and who is unlikely to be prevented from taking an original view.

EARTH TIGER

If there is one thing that the Tiger is apt to lack on occasion, it is patience, which is one of the reasons why the Chinese Tiger is inclined to get itself into some difficult situations from time-to-time. The presence of Earth in the nature has a stabilising influence, allowing a more patient and easy-going Tiger to show out under most circumstances. This is also a slightly wiser animal, or at any rate one who is more willing to learn about life from patient observation, and as a result of the advice of people who may be in the know.

Although the Earth Tiger is a slightly more sedate and steady creature than some of its relatives, this is not to infer that there is any lack of success. It might be reasonably suggested that the Earth Tiger, simply because it is so willing to look at things in a constructive manner, is more likely to be a good administrator and can build a gradual ladder to success as a result. The Earth Tiger is no less likely than the rest to be adventurous, though this is at least someone who would take a rope along on a mountain-climbing expedition. Travel could be more favoured by road or rail, rather than by water or air, but there is still the same basic Tiger need for fresh fields and pastures new.

The Earth Tiger is quite responsive to the needs and wants of those in its vicinity who may be less well off or who are in trouble of any sort. Here is an excellent and effective champion of the poor, the oppressed and the sick.

With all the Tiger tenacity in the world, but with greater common sense and good organisational skills to boot, this is a person who should not be underestimated and can usually be relied upon to work steadily towards an objective, as long as some importance can be understood concerning it.

METAL RABBIT

The standard Chinese Rabbit has many favourable attributes, though it could not be suggested that a dynamic approach to life would come top of the list. This is where Metal can be a distinct advantage to the cuddly bunny, making him or her no less loving, but at least giving more 'bite' to what can sometimes be a rather repressed nature.

The Metal Rabbit has greater perseverance, and will work long and hard to achieve its objectives in life. This may assist in furthering materialistic ends, though it must be remembered that all the Rabbit clan are inclined towards the spiritual, rather than the strictly material in life, and the Metal Rabbit is probably no exception.

There is greater passion in this Rabbit, and that means that the general love of humanity as a whole could sometimes be overthrown in favour of an intense personal love-affair of the sort that could be very positive, or quite destructive, entirely dependant on circumstances.

Once the mind of the Metal Rabbit is made up, it is very much less likely that a change of direction would be considered, which is a mile away from the indecision than mars the lives of some of this family's members.

Metal Rabbit is as kind as the day is long, and feels the needs that others have of it more keenly. It is a fact that the presence of Metal often tends to emphasise the best qualities in a less progressive sign, and certainly brings the person in question more to the foreground of life. As a result this turns out to be a very popular Rabbit, and one who is probably more reliable than some of its brothers and sisters. The magnetic and intuitive qualities of the Metal Rabbit are especially noticeable and indicate a person who would be difficult to fool.

WATER RABBIT

This really is a most pleasant variety of Rabbit to have around. Few could find fault with the affable and sensitive nature of the standard Rabbit in any case, and the addition of Water merely makes this attractive type more chatty and less inclined to sink into the odd quiet spell that could come as something of a surprise to the unenlightened. The Water Rabbit is always doing what it can to be helpful and can easily see the point of view that others put forward.

There could be at least one slight drawback here however. The Rabbit is inclined to take the line of least resistance on occasions, because it does not like to argue, or to live in a less than happy environment. The Water Rabbit is even more inclined than most to take an 'anything for a happy life' approach to most situations, and could be seen as something of a 'quitter' as a result. Any harshness of attitude to be found within the Rabbit, and this is hardly likely to be much, is removed by the sheer flexibility of Water, but you may end up with a Rabbit who will do almost anything for anyone, and one who could lose out repeatedly in a personal sense as a result.

Confusion can sometimes be the name of the game for the Water Rabbit, a fact that could rub off on the people who live with this immensely attractive, though sometimes lackadaisical character.

Romance can be a problem if this person does not learn to discriminate and insists on looking at life through rose-coloured spectacles, as it is certainly inclined to do on occasions. Unfortunately this Rabbit does not always choose very carefully and is easily fooled by a convincing 'line'. The Water Rabbit really does need the help and support of a much stronger sign if it is to function at its best in the world.

WOOD RABBIT

Here we find a very busy bunny indeed, and one that will stop at nothing to arrange a world that suits its own very exacting sensibilities. Since the Rabbit is a very co-operative type at the best of times, it should be expected that the Wood Rabbit has absorbed an even greater desire to be of use to others, and with some practicality coming from this Element, the Wood Rabbit is more than able to get things done in the material world.

A slight problem could lie in the Rabbit's need to slow things down a little, in order to bring some rest and refreshment into a life that may be more hectic than the sensitive nature can cope with. Because the Wood Rabbit insists on doing far more than any of its cousins in the warren, it is more likely than most to reach a low ebb on occasions, and even to force itself to the edge of nervous and physical exhaustion. Frequent and protracted periods of complete rest are the prescription here, together with some thought about regular meditation, good food and lots of sleep on a night.

The Wood Rabbit is undoubtedly one of the most compassionate and caring animals in the whole zoo, and people born into this combination are always ready to suspend their own lives in order to help someone who may be in trouble. There is an inbuilt practicality, together with a deep intuition that can reach inside the mind of others and look around for the cause of any upset. Once discovered, there is no lack of imagination at work to find a suitable series of solutions.

The Wood Rabbit is a dreamer its true, but these dreams are idealistic and can often be turned into solid reality with the fullness of time. The ideas of this person should not be dismissed out of hand, no matter how strange they may seem. There could be more than a grain of truth in them.

FIRE RABBIT

In purely material terms, this could be the most successful Rabbit in the warren. Generally speaking, the Rabbit is not a materialist at all, and tends to see life more in terms of how it can be happiest, rather than wondering where the next pound is coming from. Of course, the Fire Rabbit wants to be happy too, but can also turn its mind the more mundane aspects of life, altering this and tinkering with that, in order to make situations more comfortable for itself and its dependants. The Fire Rabbit is more intrepid than its cousins, and is not half so inclined to shy away from danger of any sort.

Any Rabbit has the ability to achieve its own ends as a result of psychology and manipulation, though when Fire is also present, there is more activity geared towards a goal or objective. This is a clever Rabbit, not always entirely scrupulous but at heart he or she has a fairly good idea of the way that the world really works and the Fire Rabbit can be guaranteed to play the game by its own, rather individualistic, rules.

Like the rest of the family, the Fire Rabbit really does want a peaceful life, but even a Rabbit has teeth. A naturalist once reported an incident in which a wild rabbit not only confronted, but actually defeated, a weasel, its natural enemy. This must surely have been a genuine Fire Rabbit, and gives an idea of the power latent in this type if it is provoked or threatened in any way.

The Fire Rabbit delights in throwing others off their guard but would deny strenuously ever doing such a thing, even if confronted by the facts. This Rabbit type is full of energy, loves adventure and can be a great traveller. If you see a Fire Rabbit about to embark on one of its epic journeys, you might just decide to go along, you will be certain to have fun.

EARTH RABBIT

Without any doubt, this is the kindest and most sensitive bunny of them all. The Rabbit always needs to keep one eye on the world at large, wondering how it might be possible to better help the people who are dear to it. The Earth Rabbit expands this potential, to include even people who it does not know personally. So many members of this sign and Element can be found in caring professions of one kind or another, and all of them will be just as helpful and concerned once the cares of the working day are over.

This Rabbit may not be a wanderer, and although probably happy enough to enjoy the odd foreign holiday, tends to be a happy stay-at-home, where it feels secure and within which it can build its own cheerful cocoon, which it extends around its dear family and friends. More fussy in its ways than other Rabbits, Earth makes for a good organisational nature and an excellent ability to get things right. The Earth Rabbit is quite creative, very intuitive and immensely susceptible to its surrounding.

A tendency towards worry is something that should be avoided if at all possible and over-work could create some problems if allowed to continue for protracted periods. The Earth Rabbit does need to re-charge its batteries from time to time and should not consider taking on more than one major job at the same time.

Careful with money, and concerning the finances of others too, this is a trustworthy person, capable of accepting and coping with significant responsibility and rarely letting anyone down, be they a close buddy or a complete stranger. The Earth Rabbit likes to be cuddled and requires a happy relationship in order to work at its best.

METAL DRAGON

This is one of the most explosive and potentially dominant combinations in the whole menagerie. Bear in mind that the Dragon is a creature that always knows what it wants, then add the assertive Metal Element and you have a creature that also knows how to make things happen in a big way.

The Metal Dragon will never be beaten and often treats even the most mundane situations in life as some form of competition. This can lead to a greater than average desire to see projects through to their conclusion, and since the Metal Dragon wants to do everything for itself, it can also result in a slightly isolated existence at times. Here we have a character who finds it difficult to trust others and one who may have only a few very close friends, though possibly any number of acquaintances.

The Dragon looks at the world from a fairly materialistic perspective, and the Metal Dragon even more so. Nevertheless, the casual observer should not run away with the idea that there is any lack of basic kindness or sympathy inhabiting this quite noble beast. When the sympathies of this Dragon are aroused, it can work tirelessly on behalf of less privileged people, or those who lack the dynamism that the Dragon accepts as being second-nature. However, the Metal Dragon is not one to suffer fools gladly and will soon fall out with any person who fails to put in at least a modicum of effort on his or her own behalf. This is certainly not the easiest person to understand, though realistically, what you see is what you get. This could be the reason why those who meet a Metal Dragon for the first time either establish an instant rapport with this individual, or else find him or her to be bombastic, overconfident and often rude.

WATER

WATER DRAGON

What many people find hard to take with the Dragon family as a whole is their tendency to 'tell it how it is'. To the scaly lizard this is no more than showing its natural honesty, together with the fact that the Dragon has a large enough ego to believe that its point of view is more valid than that of anyone else in the vicinity. However, the Water Dragon is a slightly different creature, possessing far more tact than would seem to be the case with other members of the clan. Although Mr or Miss Water Dragon are actually just as definite in their opinions, they are far better at getting their own way in life, simply because they can make you believe that their ideas were yours in the first place anyway.

Another slight difficulty that the Dragon experiences lies in it often being unable to explain its opinions in terms that other people can readily understand. With a slight intellectual authority, the Dragon thinks that if you are finding his or her reasoning difficult to follow, then surely the fault must lie in you. Water helps to bestow more humility, or at the very least makes it seem as if this variety of Dragon is capable of mixing happily with the masses. As a result, the Water Dragon enjoys more real friends, is able to establish a better working relationship with others and can work happily as part of a team.

Despite the softer side to this species of Dragon, it should not be assumed that any of the fire, traditionally associated with this creature, is lacking. Some say that Water puts the Dragon's fire out. In fact this is untrue, and although the Water Dragon is more inclined to use its power for the good of others, this is a dynamic Sign and Element combination nevertheless.

WOOD DRAGON

All Dragons are warm-hearted, even if they do tend to hide the fact behind a somewhat harsh exterior on occasions. Most experts would agree that the Wood Dragon is potentially the kindest of them all however, and one who is most likely to put him or herself out for those people who inhabit the same big, wide world. What makes the difference here is the natural tendency for Wood to add to the generosity of any sign, so that in this case, much of the dynamism and drive associated with the Dragon is turned outwards to the world at large.

Although probably still quite abrupt in speech, the Wood Dragon does understand the meaning of diplomacy, which is more than can be said for some of its cousins. Wood allows the Dragon to think more clearly too, so that any plan that is put into action tends to be as a result of long and serious contemplation of its possible results. Confidence to do the right thing is not lacking, but is aided by a more practical approach to problems that might be faced on the way. This is not a Dragon who would take part in any race without taking the trouble to have a look at the course first.

The Wood Dragon may know his or her limitations better than other members of the species, not that this will make them any less successful in a practical sense. On the contrary, because there is more thinking going on, there is also a greater chance of practical success, without some of the risks that attend the Dragon's life all too often.

This is a family-minded Dragon, full of warmth and charm and able to use tact and diplomacy when necessary; not exactly a living saint, but certainly no devil either. Ask this character for help and it is very unlikely that you will be refused.

FIRE DRAGON

When St George had a slight difference of opinion with a Dragon all those years ago, the offending beast was almost certainly born under the Fire Element. This is the most competitive, dynamic and enterprising Dragon of them all. Often a superb athlete, business-person and all-round dare-devil, the Fire Dragon understands life to be a series of challenges and sets out to live it accordingly. With little thought as to the outcome, this is a creature who is pleased to enter any new enterprise with complete abandon and one who will face up to each problem, as and when it arises. Fire means strength and endurance, so don't be surprised to find this character attempting an ascent of the world's highest volcano - whilst it is erupting!

There is very little that this person would shy away from, and much to be said in praise of its courage and fortitude. The only pity comes when realising that if the Fire Dragon is always right about everything - and it thinks it is, then the rest of the world of necessity must be wrong. At his or her worst, the Fire Dragon can be over-dominant, aggressive, forthright and downright bossy. Only those people who are either equally foolhardy or extremely brave would cross this individual in any way; even then the Dragon has a long memory and can usually get even when it thinks it has been wronged.

If confidence is the most important aspect of getting ahead, the Fire Dragon should be at the front of the queue all the time, though there is a foolhardy streak here that can lead to problems as well as in the direction of success and public acclaim.

This is a good combination for people in the armed forces or black-belts in karate!

EARTH DRAGON

This is a very laid-back sort of Dragon indeed, and one that spends a good deal of its time thinking about self-improvement. Like most of their kind, Earth Dragon types know where they are going in life and have a pretty good idea of what route they will have to take in order to get there. The difference between this Dragon and some of the others however is that the Earth Dragon has more patience, a far better understanding of others and significantly more self-control than some of its more dynamic cousins.

It has been suggested, and perhaps with some justification, that the Dragon individual has potentially the worst temper in the menagerie, an aspect that is also somewhat modified by the presence of stabilising Earth in the basic nature. Still, there is no lack of tenacity and every bit as much courage and fortitude as even the most aggressive of the Dragon breed. The bonus is the ability to plan carefully and then to see plans through to a logical conclusion, which removes some of the impulse and promises a better chance of overall success than might otherwise be the case.

As a partner, the Earth Dragon makes a good spouse and an indulgent, if somewhat strict parent. There is no desire on the part of individuals born with this Element to shirk responsibilites or to make light of the needs expressed by others. Always on the alert for potential difficulties, this rather slow member of the scaly clan can, when necessary, act with lightening speed. The Earth Dragon is very protective, not only of its family, but of its friends too. There may be many acquaintances in the life, though true friends are more rare in this case and one or two of them could be of a lifetime's duration. This monster is a bit of an old softy really!

METAL SNAKE

One of the basic problems with the Snake nature lies in the fact that here we have the sort of person who has the best of intentions, though not always the level of follow-through that is really needed in order to get things done in a big way. Metal can really help this situation, for although it does little to alter the Snake's affable and easy-going nature, there is definitely more bite to the personality and a greater ability to follow jobs through to their logical conclusion.

This Snake is a very passionate creature, especially in a romantic sense, and can be guaranteed to supply the right sort of chat and attention that can stimulate almost any sort of relationship.

Kind, sympathetic and understanding, the Metal Snake has the added advantage of being able to actually sort things out in a practical sense, which makes this the right sort of serpent to have around if trouble is on the horizon. In a laid-back sort of way, this is also a very brave individual, who stares danger in the face in much the same way that a cobra would face up to a mongoose, though in the case of the Metal Snake person, the opponent will usually loose any contest of strength.

There is real character evident in the case of the Metal Snake, together with deep sensitivity and a good deal of creative power to make life work out as intended. This is one of few serpents to exhibit significant ingenuity and an individual who can usually forge a successful and interesting path through life, both for itself and on account of those people who are important to it. You may find the Metal Snake having forty-winks in the sunshine, but don't be fooled into thinking that it is a lazy creature at all!

WATER SNAKE

Here we have what must be the most affable member of the Snake clan, for the Water Snake is personable, kind, laid-back and very keen to get along with all the other animals in the menagerie. At first sight this might appear to be a very good set of characteristics when thinking about living a happy life. There are drawbacks however, even if they seem to be more apparent to those dealing with the Water Snake than they are to the Snake itself. It should be remembered that the Chinese Snake is not the world's most energetic person to start with. The presence of Water in the nature could just slow down the recipient even more, so that getting the Water Snake to take any sort of action can be rather difficult.

What does stimulate a degree of movement is the search for pleasure and congenial surroundings, a state of affairs that the Water Snake finds to be of supreme importance. This is a very suave Snake, and one that always wants to look at his or her best.

There is a high degree of sensuality present in the make-up and the need to turn options of any sort over and over in the mind before any decision would be taken. If it is impossible to push the Ox, on account of its immovable strength, it is equally difficult to move the Snake, though in this case because it is the best wriggler around. The Water Snake is also a passable talker and can con its way in or out of your affections at the drop of a hat.

The Water Snake is expressive, well-intentioned, warm and apparently sincere; but it can also be a schemer, a hedonist and a romantic flirt. Which qualities you might encounter on a given day is really a matter of pot luck and could turn out to be anyone's guess!

WOOD SNAKE

It has been suggested by a few unkind souls that the Snake is a lazy sign, and that short of a bomb placed in the right physical location, little could motivate the average Snake to do almost anything. This would certainly not be the case with the Wood Snake. This variety of serpent is every bit as laid-back as any of its cousins; quiet, demure and thoughtful. The difference lies in the ability to think long and hard, and then to put in all the effort necessary to succeed in any chosen venture. The Wood Snake is generous, warm hearted and likes to take the over-view of life whenever possible.

The Snake does not often set out deliberately to change the world around it, or the people in it, though this is certainly more likely when there is Wood in the nature. This person is something of an idealist, and often follows his or her own very strong intuition. Beyond this, the Wood Snake may try to direct you down the paths that it thinks are most providential for you too. Because of this tendency, there is a small possibility that the Wood Snake person could attract the reputation for being an interfering busy-body. People who might make this accusation would do well to note that the gut-reactions of the Wood Snake often turn out to be correct.

This could be the most compassionate serpent of them all, for there is a great desire to make the world a happier place for all concerned, and a special desire to be of assistance to those people who are deprived or in need of special help. The Wood Snake can be a little more opinionated than some of its relatives in the reptile house, and is more inclined to speak its mind than any other member of the fraternity. Despite this slight drawback, the Wood Snake could turn out to be the most reliable in the end.

FIRE SNAKE

This is not the Snake to corner, or to cross in any way. Consider the natural method that the Snake-person employs in dealing with people it doesn't care for. This amounts to a refusal to recognise the existence of the individual concerned. The Fire Snake is more reactive and is apt to lash out verbally. Careful thought goes into everything that the Snake says, so the result is apt to be all the more venomous.

Here we have the 'racing Snake' if such a thing is not too much of a contradiction in terms. Certainly the Fire Snake is quicker to strike than any of its cousins, and can be guaranteed to find the target every time. These individuals lack none of the charm of their family as a whole, being every bit as demure and suave, but they are more likely to succeed in business, enjoy significantly reactive relationships and can also suffer more in the way of ill-health, should they allow tension to get the better of them. Fire Snakes have a great desire to get on with things, do not care for hypocrisy or cant and always do their best to be explicit in their own conversation.

The Fire Snake is a born adventurer, though would still probably favour travel by vehicle of some sort rather than a forced route-march through virgin forest. There is a natural physical drive here, but all Snakes are lazy in one way or another, and even the Fire Snake isn't an absolute exception.

When it comes to motivating others, this character is second-to-none. Fire makes for an infectious enthusiasm, which hardly anyone could fail to notice. With such self-belief and personal appeal, there is no wonder that the Fire Snake will have you convinced about almost anything in a flash; even if you know you are being strung-along!

EARTH SNAKE

This may turn out to be the most passive Snake of the lot, but can also be viewed as the most well-balanced and happy member of the clan. What really singles the Earth Snake out is its amazing and seemingly inexhaustible patience, for here we have a person who is quite willing to wait just as long as it takes to make things work out as he or she would wish. On the way, this Snake can cross innumerable hurdles and deal happily with any amount of problems, for to the steadfast Earth Snake, it is the end that justifies the means.

This is not at all a contradictory nature, and though the observer may not instinctively care for the slow, steady and very calculated behaviour encountered, at least it is certain that the Earth Snake will be the same tomorrow as they are today. Not that this is a boring type by any means. Earth Snake people are very creative, can be expected to be sophisticated; are good company and will lift the tone of any social situation of which they are part.

The care and concern for others is very strong, and shows itself in concerted, if steady, action to alleviate the suffering of individuals and the world at large. With a slow determination the Earth Snake has been known to amass considerable wealth, much of which may eventually be used for philanthropic projects.

Here we find an individual who takes great delight in sensual living. Good food, drink and luxury in the surroundings are all important. Confidence tends to he high, as the ego is fairly strong. Certainly not a person who could easily be coerced into doing anything that goes against the grain, and one who tends to adopt very high moral standards, or else virtually none at all.

METAL HORSE

The Horse doesn't generally stand around wondering what it should do next in life, in fact it has been suggested that this is a creature of intuition, and not really a thinker at all. This might be slightly wide of the mark because despite the instant actions and lightening speed of the Horse, the intellect is usually very strong. In the case of the Metal Horse, there is also a degree of self-discipline, born of a desire to show an unyielding and consistent face to the world at large.

The Metal Horse is just as friendly, every bit as fun-loving and quite as flirtatious as any other Horse in the herd, but he or she is also more passionate, better at thinking things through and shows greater determination than almost any other equine type. This is a Horse that will not shy away from a challenge and the courage is not merely of a cerebral sort, but exists every bit as much on a physical level too. The Metal Horse is passionate, not least of all in relationships, though this fact will not make him or her any more reliable in a relationship sense. The words of love are well-meant and the emotions run deep, the only problem being that the well could dry up at any time.

Probably stronger than any other Horse type, the Metal Horse is still inclined to burn the candle at both ends and does require plenty of time for rest and recuperation. Love and friendship are especially important and help to keep the nature stable and running along sensible lines. Where the mental attitude is right, good health and better endurance are likely to follow. Confidence seems to be greater here than it actually may be, though there is also bravado, a major factor in the lives of Horse people and something they all display to a greater or lesser degree.

WATER HORSE

Here we have a Horse which, like all of its clan, is likely to barge into almost any situation without thinking. The problem with the Water Horse is that it doesn't always know how to control a situation once it is underway. You would certainly go a long way in order to find a more diplomatic or charming Horse than this one is apt to be, though this is not the quiet and thoughtful diplomat who listens often and intervenes rarely. The Water Horse will pay heed to what you have to say, often summing up the situation as you talk. He or she will then decide on an appropriate course of action for all concerned and will be off into the sunset without so much as a 'Hi-ho Silver.'

The Water Horse has all the skills necessary to sort out a plethora of troubles. This works fine for the world at large and the only real let-down comes to the fore with the Water Horse itself. As an example: this individual is inclined to become enmeshed in some fairly demanding personal relationships. Extracating itself from such a situation would prove to be hurtful to the person concerned - and here we have the problem. The Water Horse simply cannot upset anyone intentionally, but may end up antagonising almost everyone without intending to do so.

Compromise is always possible, and there is so much latent kindness here that it is very difficult to imagine this type bearing a grudge. Such problems are legion in the life of the average Water Horse, not that this person is gullible, far from it! If there is a temper at all it is likely to be quick and verbal. Physical problems may be mentally motivated and usually include a degree of hypochondria. Detachment is an important skill to cultivate.

WOOD HORSE

One of the best members of the herd in an all-round sense, the Wood Horse is a real treasure. One of the main criticisms of Chinese Horse types lies in their tendency to be rather cold where deeper emotions are concerned, or at the very least in being unable to focus emotional commitment for more than five minutes at a time. This is not so true with the Wood Horse, who is warmer and more genuinely fixed in attitude that other members of the breed. This makes for a more lasting relationship in the case of deeper emotional attachments and might indicate that the partner of a Wood Horse will at least know where a wayward spouse might be found at any point in time.

The general interest in life is just as pronounced with the Wood Horse as with any other member of the Horse clan, so you should find that there is great enthusiasm for any new project or idea that is in the pipeline and there is certainly no lack of enthusiasm to take life by the scruff of the neck when necessary. All the same the Wood Horse is slightly better in the sphere of ethics than other Horses are inclined to be and probably also sees things from the other person's side of the fence more readily.

This is an especially influential Horse, which could be problematic if it were not for the fact that both Mr and Miss Wood Horse have the common sense and integrity to make certain that they nudge you along a sensible path in any case.

As with all Horses, this individual is bound to be nervy and needs sensitive handling on occasions if problems are not to follow. Chest and throat problems of one sort or another seem to be the most common ailment with all Horse people and it is to this area of the constitution that any undue stress generally finds its way.

FIRE HORSE

This is the leader of the herd, the alpha female or the magnificent stallion, well able to take on all potential opponents and quite willing to cross swords, intellectually of course, with almost any other Chinese animal type. There is passion, adventure and energy here in such quantities that it could make less progressive types shudder just to observe.

Although a good friend, anxious to please and very giving, the very essence of the Fire Horse nature would not be inclined to infer loyalty, which may seem to be something of a paradox when considering the Fire Horse as a champion, which he or she is quite able to be. But it is always towards fresh fields and pastures new that the Fire Horse sets its sights. Don't forget, the Horse is a roamer by inclination in any case. The presence of Fire here only makes the desire to look beyond the next horizon even stronger. As long as you are willing to trot alongside, all should be well. Only when you fail to keep up, or show some boredom with the constant need for fresh stimulus would you be left behind.

There is genuine kindness in the Fire Horse, plus a desire to do the right thing on all occasions. However, with an intellect that is keen but a nervous system that is far from indestructible, the Fire Horse expects far too much of itself and has been known to collapse with the sheer exhaustion. Because of this the best of plans may have to be modified, and in any case, the Fire Horse finds retreat to be the best form of defence if things get really hot.

Be warned, you may get a rope around the neck of this steer, though you will need strength, determination and stamina in order to hang on. The freedom of this individual takes some coming to terms with.

EARTH HORSE

Certainly the steadiest and possibly the most approachable of the Horse family, the Earth Horse is happy to stand around on the fringe of the herd and chew the grass. Not that we have a plodder here; when push comes to shove this is a fleet-footed individual who can maintain a life of high activity for considerable periods of time, but there is usually a willingness to be retiring on occasions and a desire for simplicity.

Take the prospect of a foreign holiday for example. All Horses love to travel, and the Earth Horse is no exception. Equine curiosity, plus a lively brain means that your Earth Horse will have you clambering over every ancient ruin and picturesque cliff in sight. But when the end of the day comes, you will be far less likely to be dancing frantically until dawn with this character than would be the case with other members of the herd. Your Earth Horse may sing you a pleasant holiday song, or write a poem to the glory of the sunset, but he or she is far more interested in self-improvement than in self-destruction. Because there is an inherent ability to opt for a slightly steadier existence, the Earth Horse is usually stronger in a mental sense and is far more likely to have time to see the other person's point of view.

The only drawback might be that this character is a mine of information and could give you severe earache on occasions unless you have the ability, either to marvel at the flow of words, or simply to switch yourself off now and again. The Earth Horse keeps its ears open and all information is grist to the mill, even if you personally may not be all that interested.

What you would be unlikely to find would be a kinder or more attentive lover, a more understanding parent or a better friend, for this is a gentle nag indeed!

METAL GOAT

The Goat is not the easiest person to understand in any case, and the changes that are brought to bear upon the Goat by the various Elements of Chinese Astrology are inclined to work in fairly subtle ways on this, the most enigmatic sign of them all. In the case of the Metal Goat there is a certain aloof determination that sets this type apart. Creative, passionate, complicated and mysterious he or she may be, but you will always have the impression that there is a preferred direction being taken at every stage, plus a degree of self-interest that could be mistaken for selfishness.

Remember though that all Goats are basically kind people, even if it isn't always possible to know from where the seeds of their altruism spring. The Metal Goat is no exception. You would certainly walk many a mile before encountering a more passionate individual than this one is, and here you will find a passion that can extend to just about any preferred area of life. In love the Metal Goat is steadfast and loyal, more than willing to make any sacrifice that may be necessary and always able to build a happy, comfortable environment for the family that it loves above anything.

Health-wise, the Metal Goat tends to be a fairly hardy type and though not always robust in stature can toil long and hard if necessary without any real physical suffering. The stomach may be one area to watch out for though. Excessive worry especially could result in bouts of indigestion and even ulcers if a serene and steady life-style is shunned indefinitely. Routine is fairly important in the life of the Metal Goat, but there is the chance of genuine financial gain and true independence here for the taking.

WATER GOAT

Water may well be the preferred element for the sign of the Goat, and at the very least this could turn out to be the most well-adjusted member of the clan. With Water in attendance, diplomacy, tact and sincerity come together to compliment the Goat's string of gifts, most of which come as standard on all models in any case. The Water Goat invariably has large eyes and an 'other world' expression that is immensely attractive, if something of a puzzle to more fixed types.

Getting to know the Water Goat may not be exactly easy, and many have wondered at the depth of emotion that seems to lie forever hidden behind that wistful gaze. Once you are accepted into the inner sanctum however, you have made a friend for life, and one who knows no bounds when it comes to loyalty.

This is a cultured type, happy to stroll around an art gallery or to read good literature. Although the Goat is naturally a clean type, it can take many sorts of work into its stride if to do so proves to be necessary. Most of what the Water Goat undertakes is dealt with quietly and with a conscientious determination that would be the envy of many more gregarious signs. With a slightly extravagant tendency the Water Goat definitely does have a preference for the finer things in life and would work long and hard to create a comfortable existence, both for itself and its loved ones.

This sign and element has more than its fair share of material luck, though may not be quite so fortunate in an emotional sense, since the Water Goat is inclined to be rather blind in love matches and may suffer later as a result. Happiness is invariably forthcoming eventually, thanks to patience and determination.

WOOD GOAT

The Wood Goat takes the natural sensitivity that the sign possesses naturally and makes it into an art form. This can be one of the quietest Goats of them all, an inobtrusive individual who really can walk through the waters of life without making so much as a ripple. As with any attribute this potential can be used positively, or in a negative manner. On the one hand the Wood Goat can be quietly confident, able to make decisions regarding its own life and those of other people; advising when asked and showing tremendous wisdom. Conversely, this individual could become nervy and insular to the point where some of the essential touch with the rest of humanity is lost and a hermit-like existence predominates.

There is certainly no lack of co-operation where this Goat is concerned and when at home the Wood Goat can be every bit as acquisitive and desirous of material gain as any member of the family.

In a social setting there is a demure and quiet reserve, though it is behind closed doors and in a personal relationship that this Goat comes into its own. The Wood Goat is surprisingly uninhibited in a sexual sense and may show a singular desire to make the running in such matters. In addition, we have all the components here for material success, plus a desire to get on in life that is truly breathtaking in some cases. Slowly and steadily the individual works him or herself into a position of power. Much of this can come as something of a shock when considering the sweet exterior and retiring ways of the individual under most circumstances.

All in all the Wood Goat may turn out to be the most enigmatic and surprising Goat of them all!

FIRE GOAT

If you want to see real passion, smouldering in the depths of a generally retiring nature and then suddenly bursting into flame with all the power of an exploding volcano, look no further than the direction of the Fire Goat. It can be suggested that in the case of many Chinese Animal signs, what you see is what you get. Nothing could be further from the truth in this case.

All Goats love to travel, though you would find the majority happy to improve their intellect on some cultural expedition or else soaking up the sun on a beautiful beach. In the case of the Fire Goat you would be more likely to observe him or her shooting the rapids of some raging torrent or forging a path through uncharted territory. This Goat is an adventurer, delighting in the unknown and sometimes even revelling in the positively dangerous.

The Fire Goat has a determination that knows no bounds, albeit that the casual observer is likely to be confused when confronted by the same shy, demure exterior that all of the herd seem to portray.

The Fire Goat is a sexual time-bomb, a go-getter in disguise and occasionally even a wolf in goats clothing. Always ready for action, here is an individual who can be guaranteed to get the maximum from any situation. In business this person can be extremely successful, utilising a combination of patience, hard work, genuine good luck and real know-how. Certainly not a person to be overlooked or underestimated, and the would-be adversary should be aware that there is probably no opponent more capable than this usually affable and even shy type. It may be simply because of the disarming contradictions that the Fire Goat invariably wins out in the end.

EARTH GOAT

There is patience galore in evidence with the Earth Goat, and here we find one of the quieter members of the family. Although not appearing to be particularly dominant or demanding, the Earth Goat is still likely to notch up a number of successes in life, through hard work, patience, the general good luck that Goats enjoy and with quiet determination. This Goat is very culturally minded, and can often be found inspecting fine-art or planning to improve decor around the home. The Earth Goat is not overly materialistic, but is certainly quite discerning. Why fill your house full of cheap furnishings when one, really beautiful piece would far outshine the lot? This is the mentality to be found were Earth meets the Goat and it permeates almost every aspect of the life.

The presence of Earth does little to lift the insecurity that attends this sign and indeed the Earth Goat may have more than his or her fair share of this tendency. A really secure home-life is very important, plus a steady and satisfying relationship with someone who understands how to get the most out of what is, after all, a generally retiring nature. In return the Earth Goat loves passionately and generally for life. Some confusion can attend the early life of the Earth Goat, who is generally happier once adulthood is achieved.

The health is usually fairly good, though excessive worrying can deplete the resources and might lead to stomach troubles. Food is enjoyed by the omnivorous Goat, so a little extra weight could be the price paid. Too much comfort may only add to the problem and this is definitely a sign-element combination that would do much better with plenty of exercise and a sensible routine whenever possible. A good Goat to know and on occasions a surprising individual.

METAL MONKEY

This is not the sort of Monkey who would be content to sit high in the tree-tops and throw coconuts at passers by. There is no real reserve possible when the Metal element meets the egocentric and cock-sure Monkey and this could be the most dynamic member of the troop. Metal Monkeys are always on the go, love to be the centre of attention and will not leave any stone unturned in their search for a form of personal happiness that somehow always seems to elude them. Why? Probably because the future is always receding, like the horizon to a walker. In any case, it is not the ultimate destination that is really of importance to the Metal Monkey, more the journey itself.

This is an interesting individual, highly-strung, nervy and yet exuding a confidence that may lead the unwary to believe that this person really does know what they are doing. In most situations he or she does, though the Metal Monkey is not adverse to a little bluff now and again, especially if this manoeuvres others into lending a hand. The schemes are grandiose but usually achievable, and the attitude to others is sometimes aloof though basically magnanimous. In love the Metal Monkey is attentive, passionate and giving, though there are demands to be made, not least of all the promise of fidelity, which is usually offered by the Monkey too.

The constitution tends to be fairly robust, though certainly not indestructible, and the Metal Monkey may ask too much of itself, especially at times of extreme stress. Rest would appear to be vital but is not often forthcoming. The Metal Monkey needs good friends and an active social life in order to unwind and utilise its positive mixing skills to the full, and this type is not at all happy unless it can do so.

WATER MONKEY

One of the accusations levelled at the Monkey is that it is inclined to barge its way through life, often without giving any real thought to the way that its actions have a bearing on the lives of those in its vicinity, and it is fair to say that the Monkey has a strong ego. This is not quite so true in the case of the Water Monkey, who is more diplomatic and may at least give others the impression that it is willing to listen to an alternative point of view.

The Water Monkey, like all of its family, is happy to show support for other people and in this case, can often be found in a career which is geared towards the needs of individuals if not society as a whole. Water Monkeys can be extremely generous, will always put themselves out on behalf of others and are known to be very brave when circumstances demand it. Although Water is inclined to make for softness of nature, too much in the case of some signs, it can be a good addition to the Monkey nature and usually makes for a very attractive and popular sort of individual.

Monkeys are also accused of being deceptive at times, another trait that may be somewhat mitigated in this case. All the same there is still a slight tendency for the Water Monkey to look after its own affairs with a mixture of disarming honesty and behind-the-scenes manoeuvring. A sensible life-style is demanded and usually achieved in this case, which means the Water Monkey may suffer less from the ravages of ill health later in life.

Here we have a person who is never likely to be short of good and true friends, and for everything it receives, it gives far more in return. This may be the most emotional of all Monkeys.

WOOD MONKEY

One of the greatest attributes enjoyed by Monkey people as a whole is a powerful memory. This is particularly well defined in the case of the dependable Wood Monkey, which also enjoys more than its fair share of versatility. A great lover of fashion, the Wood Monkey, male or female, is inclined to preen itself when in the public eye and will go to great lengths to buy the latest clothes.

Wood Monkeys can be tied down to some sort of routine, unlike many of the other members of the troop, and make reliable and conscientious workers. Not that the Wood Monkey is inclined to stay at the bottom of the pile for any longer than is absolutely necessary, for there is a mixture of hard-work and intelligence here that usually spells success at a reasonably early age.

Defining a role in life for the Wood Monkey would be difficult. Versatility is the middle name of both Mr and Miss in this case. This is a Sign-Element combination that loves to be of service however and one which is inclined to come before the public eye in one way or another. It possesses a highly-charged social inclination and good reasoning power. There may even be a significant level of intuition, something that other Monkeys might not have in such abundance. Do watch out though, the Wood Monkey can sometimes be a little too sensitive for its own good and is known to be slightly touchy on occasions.

As with the rest of its kind the Wood Monkey does not care for being restricted, though it can be persuaded to live a reasonably normal life, as long as the option for travel and change exist. This is almost certainly the most physically robust Monkey in the human zoo.

FIRE MONKEY

If you want to find yourself a Monkey who is more or less certain to get on in life and who will probably set the seal on doing so at a very early age, the Fire Monkey may be the man or woman who you are looking for. In addition to the many and varied qualities enjoyed by Monkey people as a whole, there is even greater strength of character here, a more pronounced sensuality and the extra dynamism needed to force through plans and schemes in the way that the Monkey is very good at doing in any case.

The Fire Monkey is hard to pin down, in fact you will have to run as a rule simply to keep alongside this energetic type. Quite often they are fitness-freaks, though that does not prevent the possibility of heart trouble or strokes if this type of person refuses to slow down a little in middle age. In fact here could be a major problem that the Fire Monkey has to deal with.

No member of this sub-clan is keen to delegate, and that means that there is often very little in the way of actual rest. The average Fire Monkey would actually do much more if only he or she insisted on a few minutes each day to meditate and collect their thoughts.

As a lover the Fire Monkey is loyal and steadfast, though perhaps not as attentive as some, mainly because their life is so busy that there is little or no time for niceties. The ego is very strong in this instance and there is absolutely no point in trying to force this person to do anything that goes remotely against the grain. Sometimes the Fire Monkey is just a little too determined and forceful for his or her own good and it takes a very strong-willed type to convince him or her of the fact. In any case it would probably be a waste of time.

EARTH MONKEY

Most Monkey people could be considered to be 'thinkers' though none more so than the more serious and contemplative Earth Monkey. In many ways this is a stable and useful combination, since the Earth Element does much to take some of the heat out of what can be a far too busy sign. There is more room for the thought processes to take a hand and so therefore less impulsive reaction.

The Earth Monkey knows what it wants from life, just as surely as all its relatives do, the only difference lies in the fact that the Earth Monkey also knows why.

Generally a considerate type, the Earth Monkey can be at home in almost any sort of gathering, though does not take kindly to injustice or deceit and will fight tenaciously to eradicate either. Earth Monkeys are kind to their loved ones and to friends, for whom they show tremendous loyalty and a desire to assist wherever possible.

More likely than many Monkeys to achieve desired objectives by slow and steady means, this individual takes time out on the way to stop and watch the flowers grow. Generosity of spirit makes the Earth Monkey a natural when it comes to charitable enterprises and a significant amount of energy is often expounded on helping humanity along a road that others often find more difficult to negotiate than does the Earth Monkey itself.

Confident and aspiring, this is an individual who most people would be pleased to have around; one who would brighten any party and who can be relied upon to control his or her powerful ego. Love and understanding come together with determination and success in the guise of this most likeable type.

METAL ROOSTER

Roosters have kind hearts and basically forgiving natures but are inclined to be rather slow on the uptake, and it is this less acceptable side of the Rooster type that might be mitigated somewhat with the presence of the Metal Element. Roosters are also deep thinkers, though many of them will only act after great forethought, something that the Metal Rooster is more likely to do without quite so much in the way of soul-searching and premeditation.

Roosters are slow to warm up in a relationship or sexual sense, though tend to be very passionate once inhibitions are finally dropped. The Metal Rooster is exactly the same, though is a more definite starter and allows the warmth of personality to permeate a greater range of possibilities. For this reason you could find the Metal Rooster easier to get to know than other chickens in the coup, and once you have made a favourable impression you should certainly find that you have a friend for life.

Although not generally a sickly type, the Metal Rooster can get through a great deal of nervous energy and this can predispose the type to all manner of hypochondriac-type complaints, as well as a few physically originated ones, particularly associated with the respiratory system and perhaps the kidneys. Fulfilment in both career and personal life could do much to keep the Metal Rooster happy and fit however, though there is also a deep dislike of confinement. All the same, the Metal Rooster can easily take on the most arduous of tasks, not to mention a tedious regime; can keep it up for weeks or months on end and then proclaim that things are really not so bad. There is certainly patience to be found here, though a little fussiness too.

WATER ROOSTER

The Rooster is a fastidious creature, always looking to improve its own lot in life but also willing to help its friends and relatives on the way. The Water Rooster is more likely to assist than any of the other Rooster types and appears to take great delight in a brand of diplomacy otherwise unknown to Roosterkind as a whole. This could make the Water Rooster a more comfortable person to be around and emphasises the more acceptable qualities of what may not be the easiest of signs to understand.

Here we have a gentle old bird and one that is far less likely to crow its own praises than some of its relatives will do. For all this the Water Rooster is keen to feather its own nest, with both Mr and Miss able to carve out a place in life for themselves and both willing to help out with the family on the way. This person is fairly versatile, not quite so fussy as some Roosters and is able to build a comfortable home where others would tend to feel reasonably comfortable.

Like all the breed, the Water Rooster lives on its nerves. Long periods of rest are important, plus the ability to travel, even if to do so sometimes goes against the primary instincts of the home-loving nature. Any harshness of attitude would tend to be washed away in the rush of Water through the nature and that means that the Water Rooster is well able to come to terms with a world that might not always fit its own standards. It is this fact primarily that sets this understanding Rooster apart from other inhabitants of the chicken-run.

There is great ability to concentrate on the job in hand in this case, even if the actions often appear less nervy and premeditated than they would in the case of other Roosters. A person of warmth and no little natural charm.

WOOD ROOSTER

There is no standard within Chinese Astrology as far as Element and Sign combinations are concerned, and yet sometimes one instinctively recognises a combination that seems to fit the bill more than any of the others. Such is the case with the Wood Rooster, which is about as true to form as any variety of Rooster might be.

The Wood Rooster is Stylish and always wants to cut a dash, even if such people tend to do so in a rather low-key sort of way. This is a frank character, not exactly outspoken, though quite willing to offer its own version of the truth if called upon to do so. The Wood Rooster can be relied upon to stick to a point of view, though is kind enough to realise that not everyone is apt to agree.

Wood Roosters are very quick on the uptake and any would-be opponent would have to get up very early in the morning to catch this character sleeping on the job. Always wanting to look behind the scenes and to make out what is really happening in life, the Wood Rooster personifies the type of curiosity that knows no bounds.

Constantly learning about life means that by middle age there is significant wisdom available, even if this is sometimes dispensed with a certain smugness that others could find rather annoying.

The Wood Rooster tends towards reasonably good health, though its slightly fussy ways can put a strain upon a nervous system that is none to strong in any case. Continual stress could just lead to bouts of hypochondria and a melancholy view of the world. With variety and plenty of interest in the life, there is sufficient strength to keep going long and hard, for the Wood Rooster is one of the best workers in the zoo.

FIRE ROOSTER

There is the best and the worst of all possible worlds available in this combination, and so much depends on the maturity and age of the person concerned when assessing just how the nature will manifest itself to the world at large.

Sufficient Fire in the nature could just tend to take away some of the more fussy and demanding qualities of the Rooster nature, though in certain circumstances, particularly if frustration attends the life of the individual, it could just accentuate them instead. Certainly this is a determined and in the main successful sort of Rooster, adept at managing its own resources and well able to look after those of its dependants who are not as adept as it is.

Here we have a complex thinker and an analytical mind that is second-to-none. All the same the Fire Rooster is far more likely to take a chance than any of its brothers or sisters in the chicken-house and can usually be relied upon to make the right choice under almost any given circumstance.

All the Fire in the world could not alter the endemic care put into life by the Rooster, so neither Mr nor Miss Fire Rooster is inclined to act on spur-of-the-moment decisions and both will be very careful in the way that they attend to their own lives, with special attention being paid to finances. This is a conversational Rooster, who loves to mix with a broad cross-section of people and can draw from the experiences of those individuals who impress it.

Concern for the under-dog tends to be fairly strong, that is if the Fire Rooster takes to the person concerned, for this is, after all, a sign and element combination that looks to its own life more than most.

EARTH ROOSTER

No Rooster is happier than on those occasions when it is allowed to wander around the yard, scratching a living for itself in the dust and just generally watching life go by. Such is the case with the Earth Rooster, a person of great charm and quiet nature.

Usually an intelligent person, though not necessarily seen as being so in a strictly academic way, the Earth Rooster gains its knowledge of life thanks to careful observation and the continuing desire to better itself. Generosity of spirit usually follows the adoption of a philosophical approach in middle life and there may also be significant religious beliefs.

There are drawbacks to the Earth Rooster. This wily bird tends to be quite fixed in attitudes, especially so if life proves to be difficult from a personal point of view. In the case of the Earth Rooster this possibility tends to be aggravated, sometimes to the point of absurdity. The result can be, in some cases, just about the most stubborn individual that you could imagine. For these reasons it is very important for the Earth Rooster to continually keep its options open, and to display a knowing flexibility of attitude as a regular daily exercise. Freedom of thought and attitude reflects on a physical level too, making the Earth Rooster less susceptible to conditions such as arthritis in later life.

Comfort and security are very important to the Earth Rooster, and there are gains to be made within long-lasting relationships. This is a very reliable type who can be trusted to remain faithful and to work hard. Perhaps it would be rather foolish to expect too much in the way of change and diversity however because this is a person who can be very much against altering a chosen path in life.

METAL DOG

Although the Dog type is inclined towards relationships, it does have the reputation of being slightly fickle and in some ways even cold towards its romantic attachments. This is really due to a fairly intellectual bias in the nature but is somewhat less evident in the case of the Metal Dog, who is likely to show more genuine passion than other members of the pack. Dogs are also accused of being indecisive on occasions, and here again the addition of Metal to the nature should help, and on the way lead to a better chance of achieving personal success.

The Metal Dog is very protective and especially brave, though not particularly in a martial sense, since this sign is not a fighter by temperament, despite its tenacity when under pressure.

There is a degree of excitability when Metal meets the Dog, which could also be interpreted as enthusiasm, particularly for new projects or the prospect of travel. You won't prevent this character from speaking his or her mind and the Metal Dog can be a tremendous gossip on occasions.

Although the Metal Dog is full of good intentions, the private lives of such individuals can sometimes prove to be good material for the average soap-opera. Complications could abound unless the Metal Dog understands that flexibility is not the same thing as a blind determination to please itself at all cost. Nevertheless here we find one of nature's diplomats and a person who takes great delight in sorting out the problems that the rest of humanity finds itself involved in from time to time. There is a strong love of life, plenty of enthusiasm and a winning smile on most occasions; very little tendency to sulk and plenty of good ideas compliment the overall nature of this most likeable of types.

WATER DOG

If diplomacy is one of the Dogs greatest attributes, then the Water Dog should be able to charm the birds down from the trees and could have warring factions eating out of each other's hands in no time at all. This individual is a natural charmer who delights in the company of interesting and witty people. Kind, sympathetic and sometimes gushingly romantic, the Water Dog is some people's cup of tea but could seem a trifle nauseating to others.

A good, if somewhat fickle, friend, the Water Dog is inclined to know literally dozens of people and probably does not care to tie itself down too much. Perhaps for this reason the Water Dog has more than its fair share of personal difficulties and is inclined to more than one romantic attachment in its life. However, this is not down to awkwardness of nature, on the contrary, this is one of the easiest people to live with that you are ever likely to meet. The real problem lies in the fact that the Water Dog is in love with the whole world, finds it easy to get to know people and makes allowances for all possible types. Water Dogs can mistake genuine affection for deep love and can come unstuck as a result.

On occasions the Water Dog can be too soft for its own good and as a result may be put upon. With the right sort of protective and advisory arm around its shoulder, the Water Dog can make a significant impression on life, though care is necessary since there is an in-built hatred of being tied down in any way.

It is a fact that the Dog type is always good to know, no matter what the ruling Element happens to be. But even beyond other Dog types there is much to be said for this happy, giving and honest-to-the-moment member of the kennel.

WOOD DOG

This is a very likeable Dog indeed and one who most people would find very difficult to fall out with. With all the flexibility that one would usually expect from the average Dog person, the addition of Wood to the nature also provides for a particularly understanding, warm and co-operative individual. There is generosity in abundance and a desire to take the line of least resistance in almost any situation. This could be part of the reason why the Wood Dog itself does not get on in life quite as quickly as it might. So busy is this person helping out the rest of humanity that it rarely has time to consider its own needs and wants as fully as should usually be the case.

There can be great anxiety at work within Wood Dog people if the nature is not serene and contemplative enough, one reason why meditation and significant periods of rest are so important to the wellbeing of this individual.

Pessimism can sometimes be a drawback, plus the inability to make an instant decision if there are a number of possibilities on offer. Relationships should be cosy and settled, though all too often the Wood Dog is inclined to act in haste and then repent at leisure.

For all the gentleness of nature, the Wood Dog is quite a courageous character at heart, can always be relied upon to help out anyone who is going through a hard time and will usually be on hand to offer timely assistance when it is needed the most.

The Wood Dog is something of a chatterbox and displays nervous energy even in the way it converses. There are never enough hours in the day for the Wood Dog to undertake everything it would wish to and there needs to be a general 'slowing down' from time to time, so that the system can settle.

FIRE DOG

There are dramatic differences of nature between the Fire Dog and some other members of the Dog family already dealt with. Even within the animal kingdom there is the sort of Dog who stands around on the edge of any problem and the kind who will wade into any situation regardless of the consequences. The Fire Dog falls neatly into the second category. Fire Dogs have an intrepid streak and although possessed of the charm that is the hallmark of their sign, Star Trek fashion, they will boldly go where nobody has gone before.

Loyal and dependable, Fire Dogs can get themselves into some real scrapes, though seem to have the ability to get themselves out of them again.

It would be almost impossible to stop the Fire Dog talking on any subject that it felt really strongly about, and such topics abound in this, one of the most socially-minded inhabitants of the kennel. A Fire Dog mate will protect its spouse and family with all the tenacity at its disposal and will never give in when it feels itself to be in the right. Not that any of this takes away from the naturally affable nature of either Mr or Miss Fire Dog, who represent some of the most likeable people to be found anywhere.

As far as general health is concerned, the Fire Dog is as prone to nervous complaints as are any of its cousins, though since it is more likely to speak its mind, there may be slightly less accumulated tension here. Confrontation is possible but is always the last line of approach to be chosen, since the Fire Dog is a natural peace-lover at heart. Fire Dog people love change, diversity and travel, and are always on the lookout for a good time, which may be part of the reason that they are so good to be around.

EARTH DOG

There is little doubt that here we have one of the most loveable Dogs in the pack, but it may turn out to be the most self-restricting too! Anyone who knows an Earth Dog person well would be bound to admit that there is affection, loyalty, compassion and understanding to be found lurking behind that noble brow.

This Dog is devoted to self-improvement and will spend large amounts of time in study, in order to make more of itself. Earth Dog people are often to be found in jobs that benefit mankind as a whole and they will work long and hard to make life more comfortable for their fellow travellers on spaceship earth.

Patience is said to be a virtue, and it is something that the Earth Dog is certainly not short of. The only real drawback is a certain tendency to be hesitant and a trifle inconsistent, both of which can really get in the way of progress. If only the Earth Dog was as positive about its own life as it is in its efforts to help out the world at large, it would probably get on very much better. Not that this is a drawback in the long-run, because the Earth Dog is likely to be helped in turn by the very large number of people who have their own reasons to be grateful.

Earth Dogs need plenty of variety in their lives, should never allow themselves to get into any sort of rut and do gain significantly by being in the company of interesting and witty types. There are fun and games to be had with this type about, but significant reflection too. All in all a character to be reckoned with, though definitely a Dog-type in whom the virtues are inclined to outweigh the few vices that do exist.

METAL PIG

This is clearly the most passionate of what is already an extremely passionate sign, and is not a character whose emotions you should tamper with lightly. If a Metal Pig falls in love with you, expect unending devotion and a loyalty that is second to none. Betray the trust that you have been allowed and then keep one eye on your back - there may be a knife on its way. Not that there need be much to fall out with the Metal Pig, unless that is you do not care for your lover to be on the possessive side. The Metal Pig sticks like glue in relationships, but it can be just a little over-clinging and is capable of significant jealousy if it thinks there is sufficient reason.

The Metal Pig is creative and even assertive on occasions; can usually be guaranteed to make a success out of its own life and often spends most of its life working on behalf of humanity, at which it excels. Both Mr and Miss Metal Pig are generally cheerful, that is if they are not engaged in some frighteningly complicated entanglement at the time, they have great perseverance and will keep going long after all the other pigs in the pen have shuffled off home.

Metal Pigs can have some very grandiose ideas, do not care to be bettered in anything and can be quite materialisic. You cannot deny that they are about, because although basically quiet at heart, if they feel strongly about anything, they may have plenty to say on the subject. They believe passionately in equality, hate prejudice of any sort and are happiest in a settled relationship.

It is easy for this person to see life in terms of balck and white, even though those around them might find the line of seperation a little more difficult to spot. However, this is a reliable sign with an even more reliable Element tagged on to it.

WATER PIG

The Water Pig is inclined to fall foul of difficult relationship problems in life, partly because it is extremely emotional by nature but also because it is extremely soft at heart and takes too many risks at the start of any sort of entanglement. Water Pigs are fairly reserved, need careful handling if they are not to suffer with nervous complaints of one sort or another and work at their very best from inside a deep, happy personal relationship. There is nothing even remotely shallow about this critter, who is willing to do almost anything for someone who it likes or considers to be a deserving case.

Miss Water Pig especially is inclined to be a little on the coy side at the start of any relationship, though don't be fooled by this for underneath that shy exterior is a porker who is brim full of passion.

Although the Water Pig prefers to conform to expected patterns, this sort of person can be quite adventurous when approached in the right way and if living with the right sort of partner. Sympathy and understanding are endemic to both sexes and there is a great need to really be of assistance to almost anyone.

It does not do to fall out with a Water Pig if you can avoid doing so. This sign is all sweetness and light as a rule but it can make a formidable enemy and will stop at nothing to get its own back if it genuinely feels that it has been wronged in any way.

The Water Pig is very astute in business, achieving its objectives in a low-key way but always winning through in the end. This individual is a good saver of money and is strongly geared towards family life, which might be the most important motivating factor of all.

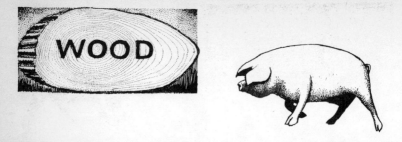

WOOD PIG

At first sight the casual observer could be forgiven for thinking that there are great similarities of nature between the Water Pig and the Wood Pig. Both show great generosity of spirit and love to help other people out. Each is shy and yet capable of great success in business. The basic difference lies in the motivation behind the nature, for whilst the Water Pig is big on sympathy, its Wood counterpart is rather better at imagining itself to be in the shoes of another person. It is the most co-operative of all the Pigs and therefore is often to be found in partnerships or in the sort of work that demands a team spirit. This also makes for a more sociable Pig-person than any of the other Elements are inclined to be.

In love the Wood Pig gives all it can towards making a good and secure relationship. It can usually be expected to be jolly and is especially happy when in the bosom of its family, the most important consideration; for though the Wood Pig seeks success, it tends to do so as a means to an end rather than as an end in itself. Always doing what it can to sort out the problems that other people manage to create for themselves, the Wood Pig can also get into some scrapes. Despite this it is practical by nature, will not necessarily take the line of least resistance and can work long and hard to get what it wants from life.

Wood Pigs make few enemies and many friends; they have the knowing knack of saying and doing the right thing, love to be in a supportive position and are inclined to shrug off any form of gratitude that comes back in their direction. If some or all of this sounds too good to be true, do remember that this character is still a Pig-type and is as likely as any of the family to show some of the less favourable traits too.

FIRE PIG

Very definitely a Pig to be reckoned with, and possibly more along the lines of a Wild Boar, that is if the naturally assertive qualities and the courage are anything to go by. The Fire Pig is extremely passionate about a range of subject matter that it finds important, and this passion also extends to the personal life of course, in which this Pig type shows more drive and sensuality than any of its more sedate cousins.

You cannot deny the importance of this character, particularly since either he or she will refuse you the right to do so. Like most Pigs the Fire type is obliging and always on the lookout for a good cause to support. There is a great desire here to make the world a better and more comfortable place for almost everyone, though there is also probably more selfishness in one or two ways than some other Pigs are likely to display. You can rely on the Fire Pig and can be certain that once something is promised, it will happen eventually.

The Fire Pig is a sensualist at heart, so it loves the good things of life and will do almost anything to make certain that there is nourishing food on the table and comfortable surroundings to live in. This sort of person also likes to bathe, to enjoy a good sex life and to dance the night away in congenial company on occasions.

The Fire Pig is kind, considerate and usually understanding; it makes a wonderful friend but a rather awkward enemy to deal with, so sensible people do all that they can to get this character on their side. At work the Fire Pig concentrates well and can usually succeed through dint of perseverance and through a determination to get things working smoothly and in an efficient manner. However, all practical aspects of life are eventually dependant on emotional stability.

EARTH PIG

This little Piggy may well go to market, and will come back with a basket filled with bargains. The Earth Pig is fairly quiet, extremely patient and only too willing to search out the things in life which it knows are good for it. It has great sensitivity, a need to better itself and a sensible view of life. It will stay away from situations of either confrontation or trouble if it possibly can and takes great delight in learning all that is on offer.

The above might lead the casual reader to believe that the Earth Pig is something of a stick-in-the-mud, but although it is true that there is patience almost beyond belief endemic in this character, there is also a slow but sure rise towards success, great intuition and a steadfast determination that even an Ox type would have to admire.

Earth in the nature tends to stabilise the more excitable qualities in almost any sign, and this it does to great effect in the case of the Pig. This makes for a home-loving type, though without some of the more dynamic passions that are typical of its Fire cousin.

The Earth Pig wants to help, like all the members of the sty, and so it makes a good and loyal friend. What is more this individual has a good idea of how to make things work out to your advantage and can easily create circumstances that benefit both itself and the people for whom it cares.

Both Mr and Miss Pig tend to be fairly attractive sorts of people and will stand out in the crowd. This fact applies to all Pig-types but is especially true in the case of the gentle, winning Earth Pig, even if this character is not at the front of the queue when it comes to singing his or her own praises.

ABOUT THE ASCENDANT

Every moment of each day, the Earth turns slowly on its axis, and because it does, it appears to those of us on the surface of the planet that the sky is passing over our heads. Astrologers of old, both in the West and the East, were aware of this fact and also observed that a fragment of the zodiac could be seen passing overhead during the hours of darkness. They believed that the sign of the zodiac occupying the eastern horizon at the time of any person's birth would have a significant part to play in the ultimate character of that individual. This zodiac sign is known as the Ascending or Rising sign.

The Earth's relationship with the stars is a complex one, and in Western Astrology the Ascending Sign is not easy to establish. However, the Chinese were able to split the day equally and to attribute a part of it to each zodiac sign, so it is not especially difficult to work out which one you fall within, of course assuming that you have some knowledge of your time of birth. All you have to do in order to discover your Chinese Ascendant is to look at the table on the following page.

Each hour of the day is listed, together with the Chinese Zodiac Sign which is said to rule it. Once you have discovered your Ascending Sign, you can refer to the pages that follow to discover the interpretation of your animal Ascendant.

Most Astrologers believe that the Ascendant will make itself known in the way that you appear to other people in your day-to-day life. Don't forget though that your Animal Year and also your Moon Sign will also have a significant bearing on your nature. It is this combination of influences that is so important when it comes to assessing your nature.

COMPARISON CHART

Many readers will also be interested in the connection between Chinese and Western Astrology. It's true that every one of the Chinese signs does have a more familiar Western counterpart, though what most people consider their Astrological sign, or 'Sun Sign' in the West, becomes the 'Moon Sign' in Chinese Astrology. Overleaf is a useful comparison table, so that you can compare the signs in both systems of Astrology.

CHINESE ASCENDANT TABLE

HOUR OF BIRTH	SIGN	HOUR OF BIRTH	SIGN
1am. to 2am.	OX	2am. to 3am.	OX
3am. to 4am.	TIGER	4am. to 5am.	TIGER
5am. to 6am.	RABBIT	6am. to 7am.	RABBIT
7am. to 8am.	DRAGON	8am. to 9am.	DRAGON
9am. to 10am.	SNAKE	10am. to 11am.	SNAKE
11am. to 12am.	HORSE	12am. to 1pm.	HORSE
1pm. to 2pm.	GOAT	2pm. to 3pm.	GOAT
3pm. to 4pm.	MONKEY	4pm. to 5pm.	MONKEY
5pm. to 6pm.	ROOSTER	6pm. to 7pm.	ROOSTER
7pm. to 8pm.	DOG	8pm. to 9pm.	DOG
9pm. to 10pm.	PIG	10pm. to 11pm.	PIG
11pm. to 12pm.	RAT	12pm. to 1am.	RAT

CHINESE SIGNS AND WESTERN COUNTERPARTS

CHINESE SIGN	WESTERN SIGN
DRAGON	ARIES
SNAKE	TAURUS
HORSE	GEMINI
GOAT	CANCER
MONKEY	LEO
ROOSTER	VIRGO
DOG	LIBRA
PIG	SCORPIO
RAT	SAGITTARIUS
OX	CAPRICORN
TIGER	AQUARIUS
RABBIT	PISCES

RAT ASCENDANT

Since the Ascendant has a tremendous bearing on the way that you display yourself to the world at large, it's a fair bet that whatever your Animal Year Sign, you are an outgoing person, anxious to please and generally fun to have around. You may not be the world's most ethical type though such is the vivacity and appeal of your nature that you would be likely to get away with almost anything.

There is no doubting your abilities in life, though how well you put them into practice is of course partially dependant on your Animal Year Sign. You are probably quite chatty, and enjoy the company of interesting and witty people. It would be difficult for others to pull the wool over your eyes and you may show a significant temper on those rare occasions that you consider yourself to be under attack. You don't take kindly to being made a fool of and yet you can be a tremendous practical joker yourself.

Whatever you undertake is likely to be seen through to the end, with an enviable brand of talent, bravado and good old-fashioned bluff. Not that this prevents your success in life being very real. Many Rat types are self-made individuals and all love the cut and thrust of everyday life. Rat's are sporting, even though they are inclined to do only what they have to on the way to achieving any objective. This fact is not on account of any inherent lazy streak but is responsive to the Rat's desire for variety, for this individual can tire easily if forced to follow the same routine for any length of time.

In love, the Rat Ascendant individual is attentive and kind. There is a degree of loyalty here too, just as long as things are working out to the Rat's satisfaction. However, the Rat can be inclined to variety in relationships.

OX ASCENDANT

Right from the start it should be said that you have little difficulty establishing a base for real success in your life, even if this process takes rather longer to achieve in your case than it might with the aid of other, more apparently dynamic, Chinese Signs. It isn't your way to rush your fences, or to force issues through that would respond better to patience and careful planning. All the same, once you have made up your mind to any particular course of action, nothing and nobody would be able to prevent you from getting your own way.

Comfort and security are both extremely important to you, and there is nothing that you desire more than a settled home-life and a family who adore you. Conformity is all to the gentle, plodding Ox, who is adverse to taking risks of any sort and really wants to have as peaceful a life as proves to be possible. All the same you have great determination and an iron will, which means that only the most foolhardy sort of individual is likely to cross you.

There is every chance that you know yourself fairly well. You are a no-nonsense sort of character, though full of charm, very artistic and always anxious to please. It's a fair bet that your friends would readily turn to you for the invaluable advice that you can offer, since they recognise you as being eminently sensible and a tower of strength to anyone who happens to be in trouble. Being of a practical nature, you can get things done around the house and instinctively know what looks and feels right.

Despite all the above you can seem to be a rather strange sort of individual to those people who do not know you all that well and you do need to do everything in your own careful and steady way.

TIGER ASCENDANT

There is something especially appealing about Tiger Ascendant people. Perhaps it is the very unpredictable side to the nature that makes these individuals so refreshing to have around, together with a love of freedom that makes them so desirous of a world that constantly brings surprises along to brighten up even the most gloomy of days. If you enjoy this Ascendant you can be certain that you will always be surrounded by good friends and that you can gain support for your many plans and ideas, no matter how outlandish those around you consider them to be.

You are by nature a very liberated sort of individual, just how much so is partly dependant on other aspects of your Animal make-up. Whatever your Animal Year and Moon, kindness is your middle name and you would not dream of doing anyone a bad turn if it was possible to help them in some way. It's true that you can sometimes be a little reckless, though never in a destructive way. Few circumstances would hold you back and perhaps the only real restricting influence is created when the world, or certain individuals, attempt to thwart you in your endeavours.

Having the sign of the Tiger on your Ascendant allows you a slightly more reckless quality than might be emphasised by other aspects of your nature, and that means that you are willing to take a significant risk if you think that the end will justify the means. Few could predict the way that your mind works and once they know you, even fewer would want to try. Although you are socially inclined in some ways, you can also be very much of a loner, after all Tigers are famous for walking alone much of the time. Just like this fearsome cat you have great strength, but generally speaking you keep it in reserve.

RABBIT ASCENDANT

Rabbit people are some of the most peaceful and happy creatures to be found anywhere in the Chinese Zoo, a fact that tends to apply no matter what other signs are present in the individual, for although the Rabbit is not a dynamic sign, it does have the ability to make its presence felt under almost any circumstance.

Rabbit people are refined, so chances are that you would be welcome at almost any sort of gathering or function. You can be relied upon to behave yourself and although not the most noisy member of the menagerie, you do have the ability to say more or less the right thing on any given occasion. With a dislike of arguments or general upset of any sort, you would probably shy away from confrontation and tend to get your own way by more subtle means than would be available to many of your brother and sister signs.

When dealing with the world at large it should be remembered that you have a great ability to catch others off their guard. With this gift, and a mixture of subtlety and diplomacy, you can usually bring situations round to your way of thinking, and may even fool people who have ten times your natural aggression. Some people might see you as being a little aloof, especially when it comes to looking after your own. The fact is that you can feather your own nest extremely well, a consideration that could surprise those individuals who do not have the ability to understand the complexities of your difficult sign.

Comfort is an important factor in your life, so you will want harmonious and co-ordinated surroundings, take delight in pleasant scenery and may not willingly travel all that far from home.

DRAGON ASCENDANT

Put out the flags and blow a fanfare on the trumpets - the majestic Dragon is around. No matter what your Animal Year Sign may be, you cannot have failed to notice already that you cause something of a stir wherever you go, or that people either love or hate you, probably with no inbetween. It's like that if you are a Dragon and has been so throughout history. Times don't really change, so in some places you will be welcomed with open arms for your frank and fearless approach to life, whilst in others you will receive a cooler response - probably because you can be just a little bossy on occasions!

If you are a true, died-in-the-wool Dragon, you really will not care what opinion the world at large has of you, though this cannot be put down exclusively to arrogance on your part. It's simply that you know where you are going and the best way to get there. You show great ambition, versatility, endurance and tremendous courage. Your method of thinking is progressive and interesting; those people who take to your brand of nature really do think that you are the tops and would do almost anything to keep you smiling, which isn't too hard anyway.

Although you tend to make a success of your life, in a practical sense at least, you are very ethical in the way that you go about things, which is probably why even those individuals who cannot really take to you as a friend do have a somewhat grudging respect for the way you go about achieving your objectives. Adversity is something that you do not fear and you can fight back against almost any set-back to gain the upper-hand on the way towards any destination that seems important at the time. Confidence is the greatest weapon in your armoury, though you may not be quite as powerful as you think and like everyone else in the zoo you do need a little rest occasionally.

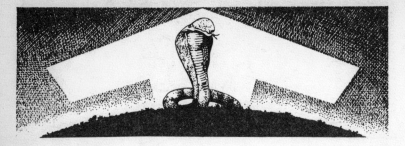

SNAKE ASCENDANT

Here we have a creature who just refuses to be rushed, though from the offset it should be remembered that the snake can, when provoked, strike with lightening speed, so the Snake Ascendant individual should never be underestimated. This is a person of great charm and good breeding - the sort of individual who you could take just about anywhere, in the certain knowledge that they will know how to act to their own, and your, complete satisfaction. True, the Snake person does not like to be cornered or intimidated, though under most circumstances, the Snake is a happy-go-lucky type and enjoys the prospect of a good time.

If you were born with the Snake Ascending, you have all the natural attributes brought to bear on the personality by this most charming and attractive Chinese Sign. You can expect to have many acquaintances and a few really good life-long friends. You probably show a respect for fashion that borders on an obsession and will enjoy the good things in life, which include food and drink, luxury generally, and the chance to travel to exotic locations. Some people would find you to be quite profound and perhaps a little difficult to understand, so it is good for you and them if you explain yourself as carefully as your rather closed nature allows. This might mean going to greater lengths than sometimes seems necessary to put your point of view and certainly does not allow for a little sulking, which is not out of the question if you feel that you have been misunderstood.

Although you can be fairly quiet by nature, you are inclined to be something of a socialite. You are pleased to be noticed, the more so because you always take the trouble to look smart and don't care for being seen in public unless prepared.

HORSE ASCENDANT

How could you be missed? There is no doubt about it, you come from one of the most outgoing and attractive enclosures in the zoo. You stand out in a crowd and do not mind the fact in the least. The reason is that you long for attention and can become very bored if you don't get it. The ideas which you are always expounding are tinged with genius on occasions, even if you are also capable of making some rash and foolish decisions from time to time.

In love you are inclined to be something of a flirt and members of the opposite sex probably consider you to be full of sex-appeal. This can lead you into trouble at some stage in your life, unless you have the stability of a romantic partnership that you consider to be satisfying, both personally and intellectually. Friendships tend to be many and varied. Horse types are known to mix with a rather strange cross-section of people and can usually be relied upon to offer the right sort of advice to those who are in trouble or in need of special support.

Perhaps the most important facet of your nature is your instinctive ability to entertain. Even though you are subject to ups and downs, you are rarely out of sorts for long and will usually be found where there is laughter and an ability to make the best of even difficult circumstances. This is one of the reasons why you are so loved by practically everyone you know, even those people who would care for you rather less than they do, if only it was possible!

You certainly do not care for confinement of any sort, love to be able to wander more or less wherever you want and find great joy in travel. Your animal namesake is a creature of rolling plains and wide open spaces; and you are really no different yourself.

GOAT ASCENDANT

You certainly are not the most outgoing or noisy person to be found at large, though this does not mean that you fail to stand out in a crowd, or that you are going to be at the back of the queue when it comes to getting what you want from life. On the contrary, in your slow, steady and often gentle way you can really make an impression, find it relatively easy to get your own way and give a good account of yourself in any given situation.

It's true that you have an extravagant streak and that you are drawn towards luxury in almost all its forms. Despite this you are not at all materialistic and are happy to go without in order to support a cause that you really believe in. Goats are often to be found supporting less well-blessed types and your patience is such that you can remain considerate of people who may have been rejected by other well-meaning agencies. You are naturally creative, so that if you do not choose to spend your life in a career that involves helping humanity as a whole, you could be drawn towards an artistic pursuit. Whatever you undertake, you are capable of working long and hard to achieve your objectives, you can plan carefully and do not object to waiting in order to get what you want from life.

It is often suggested that Goats are lucky people, though this would tend to ignore the Goat's ability to be frugal and to only take chances when the odds are looking especially favourable. It is true however that you can be very insecure on occasions and do need considerable encouragement to take emotional chances, especially if you have been through a painful experience in the past. Once committed to a relationship of a personal nature you are capable of being very uninhibited when you feel comfortable.

MONKEY ASCENDANT

The Monkey is a very clever creature some say the most astute in the Zoo, so don't be surprised if you get on well in life, after all your Monkey Ascendant is there to help you along. Many Eastern cultures consider the Monkey to be the leader of all other animals, and certainly this astute character figures prominently when it comes to steering other human animals in whatever direction they see fit. Not that this makes you an overt user of others, because at your best you will always have their own interests at heart too.

One of the strongest points of your nature is your undeniable versatility, for most Monkey types could turn their hands to almost anything. Whatever you do decide to undertake is dealt with in the same cheerful and efficient manner, though you can become bored with routine and like as much diversity in your life as possible. Because of this fact you can be accused of being fickle on occasions, especially when young. However, most Monkey types grow in confidence and in endurance, which is why so many of them manage to carve out a niche for themselves in one area or another.

Emotionally speaking you are quite capable of being rather unsettled, whilst in a sexual and relationship sense you are undoubtedly provocative and generally attractive to members of the opposite sex. You like to look your best under any given circumstance and do all you can to remain attractive throughout your middle years and beyond. You are not born of an Ascendant that particularly relishes growing old however and will always do what you can to remain in touch, and in fashion. Your memory is good and you can amass a mine of information simply by keeping your ears open. This is made easier because you show an interest in almost anything.

ROOSTER ASCENDANT

The greatest gift you bring to the world, both for your own sake and on behalf of the many people who benefit from your kindness, is a great consistency. However, that which is your strongest point invariably turns out to be the weakest too and you have to be especially careful to make certain that you include flexibility in your day to day life if you are not to become far too set in your ways.

You are a stylish old bird and like to be at your best in any situation. With an above average intelligence, and an ability to find the right words to make yourself understood, there are very few people who would fail to understand what you are trying to say to them. Personality-wise you are confident and understanding, able to make the best of difficult situations and are always anxious to see things from the other person's point of view, even if you don't always manage to understand what that might be. No Rooster suffers fools gladly and so you may not appear to be the most patient person in the world. Quite often you find it easier to do something for yourself than to trust it to other people and even this facet of your nature can be slightly irritating to the people who live either with you, or in close proximity.

In terms of your opinions you are forthright and usually are correct in the way that you deal with the world at large. Intuition is strong in your nature, so that you often have a very good idea concerning the way any project or idea is likely to work out. All Roosters are complex thinkers and it is true that you can over-complicate things on occasions, even though by dint of perseverance you usually get to your chosen destination in the end. Constitutionally you are strong, though there is a tendency towards hypochondria and a nervy side to your nature.

DOG ASCENDANT

There is little doubt that you are fun to have around, and you tend to cheer up almost any group or association of people with whom you come into contact. As a Dog Ascendant person you are naturally excitable, and inclined to speak your mind under most circumstances, despite the fact that you have a naturally diplomatic stance to rival that found anywhere else in the menagerie. Popularity is not something that you have to go out looking for, on the contrary, you only have to put in an appearance to discover how much people think about you. Why? Because you are fun to have around and can enliven any flagging gathering simply by being present.

Like the Dog after which your Ascendant sign is named you are naturally loyal and protective, inclined to be especially kind to those you take to, but you are known to flit about a little and so may not be the most constant type around in a year by year sense. This is not to infer that friends are of little real value to you, on the contrary you would do almost anything for an individual who you see as being important. Understanding what makes others tick is not difficult in your case and you are a good judge of character, unless that is you are involved with someone on a personal level, in which case your emotions tend to rule your intellect.

Anxiety is your worst enemy and all people enjoying a Dog content to their astrological make-up should practice the art of meditation. This tends to slow down the nervous system and gives the individual the chance to look at things from a more sedate stand-point - something that the Dog really needs to do. There is a quiet side to your nature and you are known to be fairly demure. If life really kicks you in the teeth you show a slight tendency to become rather cynical.

PIG ASCENDANT

You can be a fairly complex character, even though you might be personally surprised to learn that you are, and this is the reason why not everyone you come across understands you immediately. However, once people really learn what makes you tick you are liable to make reliable, life-long friends and only really feel secure yourself when you know that there are people around who will back you up. The love that you have for home and family is legendary and the family unit is of significant importance in your view of life. A secure marital relationship suits you best and the divorce rate amongst Pigs tends to be very low.

Although sensual by nature you can also be fairly coy, which often gives people the wrong impression about the sort of person that you really are. But for all your personal attributes emotionally, you are also extremely astute and would not easily allow the wool to be pulled over your eyes. Part of the explanations for this state of affairs lies in your keen perception and strong intuition. You can usually guess what the nature of any given individual is likely to be and once you have made up your mind, you rarely change it.

Most Pigs are very brave and are also known to be charitable by inclination. Working for the good of mankind comes as second nature to your sign and so it is not surprising to discover that there are many Pig individuals in the caring professions. It is important for you to feel wanted and so you do all that you can to assist those around you in an advisory as well as in a practical way. Confidence may not be your strong-point in some respects, though when it comes to defending any individual you care about, you can be very brave, extremely tenacious and undeniably loyal.

COMPATIBILITY

In all forms of astrology it is useful to know what signs of the zodiac your own birth sign is likely to get along with. The Chinese are no exception with this regard, and especially where love is concerned, have always been careful to look at the way other signs relate to their own. Of course it makes sense to also bear in mind your Ascendant and Moon Sign when assessing your chances of hitting it off with any other person.

Below you will find a chart which makes it simple for you to find the comparison between any two Chinese signs, Look for your own sign down the left-hand side of the chart, and the sign you want to compare it with along the top. Where the two coincide you will see a page number, Turn to that page in the following section to learn about Chinese Animal compatibility.

	Rat	Ox	Tig	Rab	Dra	Sna	Hor	Goa	Mon	Roo	Dog	Pig
RAT	158	158	158	159	159	159	160	160	160	161	161	161
OX	158	162	162	162	163	163	163	164	164	164	165	165
TIG	158	162	165	166	166	166	167	167	167	168	168	168
RAB	159	162	166	169	169	169	170	170	170	171	171	171
DRA	159	163	166	169	172	172	172	173	173	173	174	174
SNA	159	163	166	169	172	174	175	175	175	176	176	176
HOR	160	163	167	170	172	175	177	177	177	178	178	178
GOA	160	164	167	170	173	175	177	179	179	179	180	180
MON	160	164	167	170	173	175	177	179	180	181	181	181
ROO	161	164	168	171	173	176	178	179	181	182	182	182
DOG	161	165	168	171	174	176	178	180	181	182	183	183
PIG	161	165	168	171	174	176	178	180	181	182	183	183

RAT MEETS RAT

This is a potentially explosive combination, especially since the Rat is inclined to want its own way so much of the time. Although a very sociable type, the Rat person does want to be the centre of attraction and might not be too happy sharing the limelight with a competitor. However this would certainly be a meeting of minds and indicates a cerebral relationship that could be fairly stimulating for both parties. The Rat wants to be helpful and is very fond of its home and family, yet it also needs to be sociable and at least with this combination there would be few arguments about the merits of staying in as against tripping the light-fantastic. Both partners will be along for the outing!

RAT MEETS OX

Here we have two radically different outlooks on life, though that is not to infer that this potential relationship is a non-starter; on the contrary, the fast, explosive Rat makes an ideal comparison to the slow, plodding Ox, which could in itself be a recipe for success. In this partnership it is possible for the Ox to earth-out some of the more high-flying qualities of the Rat, making for a more considered response and better powers of concentration. Rats do need to be slowed down from time to time and respond well to the bovine attitude to life. Meanwhile, the gregarious Rat can do much to move the more sedate Ox and can help to bring a little excitement to life.

RAT MEETS TIGER

An interesting combination this, but it does not get many marks for a number of reasons. Both these signs want to have their own way and yet they do so for radically different reasons. The Tiger, although sociable, always walks alone in any case, and has an original and often unique view of life. Rats want to be out and about, love the cut and thrust of inter-action and a party atmosphere, whilst Tigers could well be anxious to be striding off along some rocky mountain range. It's true that both signs are humanitarian by nature and that they enjoy being well thought of, and yet there is a certain reserve about the Tiger that the Rat might find awkward.

RAT MEETS RABBIT

The Rabbit is such a mild-mannered sort of individual that the subtlety of this quiet individual could be completely lost in a union with the ever-sociable and gregarious Rat. There would certainly be much love in evidence, even though it may show itself in a number of different ways. It's possible that the Rabbit would relish the protective arm around its shoulders that aRat about the house promises, yet if it came to an argument of any sort, difficulties would be likely, since the Rat knows how to express its ideas, even emotional ones. whereas the more reclusive Rabbit does not. For real success here the Rabbit must develop some muscle.

RAT MEETS DRAGON

All things considered this is not a bad match. Only the Rat could hold its own fully against the majestic importance of the Dragon, whilst the Dragon would get a kick from the stimulation, mental and physical, that comes its way via the Rat. There would never be silences in a house where these two were sharing the mortgage, and with the potential success of both signs there should be plenty of money coming in to pay the bills. Arguments would be of immense size and scale, for neither of these creatures relishes being beaten. Still, there would be little malice and a common forgiveness that could mean making up would be a memorable experience in itself. Confrontation might be avoided altogether once the Rat and the Dragon really come to terms with their respective roles.

RAT MEETS SNAKE

If there is one thing that would get on the nerves of the Rat in this relationship it is the fact that the Snake simply refuses to be rushed, is inclined to take life at reptile pace and doesn't have the same desire for personal success that is endemic to the Rat. Where the Snake can stay at home and look after things in its own inimitable way, all should be well, and the only real problem arises when things are the other way round. Meanwhile the Snake would find it difficult to come to terms with the pace of life demanded by the busy and always thinking Rat.

RAT MEETS HORSE

These two are opposites in every sense of the word, and particularly so in an asotrological sense, and yet there are so many similarities that they just might manage to make a go of things, even if the reasoning behind their chosen life-style is not the same. Both signs are genuinely gregarious and love the company of others. Each is clever in its own way and could contribute to the flow of knowledge that typifies the coming-together of the Rat and the Horse. This is a social match, based primarily on trust - it has to be, because both signs are wanderers by nature! Comfort and security would not be especially important.

RAT MEETS GOAT

The Goat is a stay-at-home, or else the sort of person who really wants to see the world - warts and all. There might be a fundamental difference here, for although the Rat loves to get out and about too, you are more likely to find it in a disco than forging a path through the Amazonian rain forest. The Rat is a social climber, whilst if the Goat climbs anything at all it is likely to be a precipitous rock-face. In between adventures the Goat loves to stay at home and toast its toes by the fire. It is a good home-maker and needs family ties. These are not so necessary for the Rat, who sees the world as its family.

RAT MEETS MONKEY

There are enough similarities here to make for a good relationship on most levels. Not least of all the fact that both these signs have a significant ego and understand what it means to take life by the scruff of the neck and make it do what you want. There is clearly a competitive edge to this pairing and so some arguments are more likely than not.

Fun and games attend this relationship and it's fair to say that both signs like to have a good time. Comfort and security would appear to be bottom of the list of priorities, though the Rat and the Monkey may have a good and substantial home, for both enjoy good earning power and are not afraid to spend cash when it proves to be to their common advantage. All the same there could be fireworks occasionally with this match.

RAT MEETS ROOSTER

A confusing possibility this one, though possibly none the worse for that. It's true that the Rat does not care for being nagged and it is also fair to say that, at its worst, the Rooster is the best nagger of them all. Not that this is necessarily a bad thing, since the capricious Rat often responds well to a little gentle persuasion. The Rooster is looking for a cause, and trying to organise a typical Rat type would be cause enough for anyone in a single lifetime. Meanwhile the Rat finds that it does not have to worry about certain fundamentals of life for which it has neither the time nor the inclination. If as a result both parties get what they are after, the circle of necessity is closed and the possibility of happiness stands waiting this pair.

RAT MEETS DOG

Dog people are generally so affable that they are to be found living happily with just about any other animal in the Chinese zoo, though this could turn out to be one of the better possible combinations, not to mention one that brings a lively interplay and a meeting of minds. This would certainly not be a relationship existing primarily on a physical level, though bearing in mind the fertile imagination of both signs even this aspect of life is grist to the mill. These types think, and because they do can come up with some useful mutual ideas. A refreshing combination this, though lacking stability.

RAT MEETS PIG

At first sight it might appear that these individuals do not have very much in common, and a second glance may only serve to confirm the suspicion. Rats and Pigs are after very different things in life; the Rat with its superficiality and the Pig, to whom intensity is a way of life. It isn't that they would find it impossible to rub along together tollerably well if they had to do so, since both signs can be very personable. More likely is the fact that they would never be attracted to each other in the first place, at least not in a personal sense. The Rat would always feel that the Pig lived in realms that it did not understand, whilst the Pig may be inclined to find the Rat to be 'too clever by half'.

OX MEETS OX

If like-poles were ever to attract in this world, then this might prove to be the best of all relationships. Until that distant time it would probably be fair to say that there would be too many similarities to make this a going concern. The home occupied by two Ox types would be neat and orderly. Arguments would be a rare occurrence and peace would probably reign for most of the time. If this sounds a little like paradise, then do bear in mind that most people also require a little fire in their lives,even the slow and steady Ox. This is usually supplied by a more dynamic partner of the type favoured by Ox people as a rule. Without it life might be very dull.

OX MEETS TIGER

There is a good chance that this combination will have distinct advantages for both partners, not least of all because the Tiger has a good deal more get-up-and-go than the Ox, and since Ox types definitley do want to be more dynamic than providence might have made them by chance, they can gain significantly by having the original and quite adventurous Tiger close at hand. Looking at things from the other side of the coin, the Tiger is sometimes too high-flying for its own good and responds very well to the reliable Ox, who doesn't mind making certain that there are clean clothes to wear!

OX MEETS RABBIT

Here we have two of the kindest people to be found in a month of Sundays. The only problem is that they stand a good chance of boring each other to death. The difficulty is that both the Ox and the Rabbit are basically quiet people, not given to a riotous life and happy to stay home most of the time. Basics will be taken care of by both parties and the home made together by the Ox and the Rabbit would be cosy and warm. Some problem could be experienced when it comes to the stubborn streak enjoyed by the Ox, which may not be easily understood by the Rabbit, who tends to be far more flexible and is generally happy to go with the flow. Personality-wise, there is little to separate these two in the eyes of the world at large and the match could just work.

OX MEETS DRAGON

It might appear at first sight that here we have a perfect match. After all, the naturally quiet ways of the Ox could be seen as the perfect counter-balance for the more volatile Dragon. In some ways this is true, but it should also be remembered that the Dragon seeks to push, both situations and people! Herein lies the basic problem, because the sedate Ox will not be budged one inch further than it wants to go, added to which there is a stubborn streak here that knows no equal in the whole Chinese zoo. All the same, this match cannot be dismissed as being of no benefit to either party. Significant material success usually attends this union, since both parties are good and hard workers.

OX MEETS SNAKE

Without doubt this is a good and generally happy union. True, life in this household may lack a little sparkle, at least when judged from the point-of-view of more gregarious types, but then neither the Ox nor the Snake are looking for too much in the way of excitement. Both are happy to work hard when circumstances indicate it is necessary to do so, though the Snake and the Ox are just as likely to lie together in the garden and soak up the sunshine. Family matters are important here and genuine love will attend the union. Beware a mutual stubborn streak!

OX MEETS HORSE

Classical astrology would argue against this match, and yet this could be a meeting of opposites that is a very workable commodity. True, the Ox wants to have its own way a good deal of the time, but is inclined to be very susceptible to flattery, which just happens to be the stock-in-trade of the Horse. If any individual can get the most out of the Ox, it must surely be the cheerful, happy-go-lucky Horse, who doesn't mind in the least that its partner is not so effervesant or jolly. Why? Because the last thing that the Horse is looking for is a rival. Meanwhile the Ox will wash the clothes and keep the house tidy and will be constantly told by its Horse partner just how wonderful it is. And why not? It's probably the truth!

OX MEETS GOAT

This union might work very well in the confines of a monestary, especially if it were a contemplative order. Both parties are naturally quiet and not given to speaking their minds, at least not unless sorely provoked into doing so. The Goat is a very sensitive type, and may not take kindly to the slightly brusque manner of the Ox, especially when things are not going its own way. This is not an entirely hopeless case, and the only real problem is likely to be a lack of interest in life when it comes to excitement. You probably would not see this pair winning a disco dancing competition or walking across Africa together. Chances are that they will be at home, decorating the kitchen - again!

OX MEETS MONKEY

Here we have a very good friendship in the making, but this could be a million miles away from a romantic attachment of life-long proportions. Of course there are exceptions that prove every rule and it could just be that there is an understanding here that indicates happiness of a sort. The Monkey is a forceful type by inclination and could on occasion come up against the immovability of the Ox, though since the Monkey doesn't really care for people who allow it to have its own way all the time, even this could be a blessing in disguise. All in all we have to see this union as being a definite possibility.

OX MEETS ROOSTER

If you are on your way to visit this pair at home, make certain that you wipe your feet and don't think about dropping any crumbs on the carpet. This is probably the most tidy union in the menagerie. The Ox-Rooster couple are very happy in each others' company and would rarely cross swords. Conversely, there could be a sort of in-built sterility to the relationship, especially on those occasions when neither party has anything particular to offer. There is a good capacity for home building and for looking after money. If there is a communicator here it is likely to be the Rooster, though since neither sign is a leader by inclination it could appear sometimes that the partnership lacks a little direction. Both signs are capable of much love.

OX MEETS DOG

Tung Jen considers this to be a potentially good match, mainly because the Dog is adaptable enough to make allowances for the sedentary ways of the Ox. Not that this is a one-way street. The Dog is a charming character, though not the most practical sort of person you would ever meet. The Ox is a born organiser, loves to be responsible for others, and though constantly taking the Dog to task for being so hopeless in some respects, would tend to do so with a sense of love and a sardonic smile. There is nothing the Ox wants more than to be needed, whilst the free-wheeling Dog finds a solid base on which to place its dreams and ideals. A hopeful, warm and sincere attachment is in the making when the Ox and the Dog come together.

OX MEETS PIG

Certain attachments bring out particular traits in specific signs, and especially so if the quality is shared by both parties. That's why sensuality becomes so much a part of this union. Eating, sleeping, bathing and making love will all be very important in this household, and it will often be a competition as to who can manage the most of each! Certainly in the food department, this would be an unhappy pair if on a diet, and both signs really do crave for the luxury that they adore. Practically this might be a reasonably good union.

TIGER MEETS TIGER

What an unusual relationship is in the making here. The Tiger, although appearing generally definite to the world at large, really has no clue where it is coming from, or where it might be headed - perhaps two Tigers together don't know either, or care very much for that matter. Although gregarious and charming, the Tiger is inclined to walk alone and often revels in its eccentricities. All the more reason to suppose that the Tiger-Tiger household would be strange and quite unfathomable to the unprepared outsider. You could find this pair setting up house in a jungle clearing, a squat or a commune. They are likely to have children who turn out to be every bit as original as they are and always create happiness.

TIGER MEETS RABBIT

This might turn out to be a reasonably good match in some ways, especially since both the Tiger and the Rabbit tend to be very understanding types in their own very different ways. There could be one or two problems for the poor Rabbit person however, since this is a sign that needs to know where it stands in a relationship, always difficult when living with the rather changeable Tiger. However, Rabbits are quite intuitive and can usually be relied upon to make allowances for natures that are sometimes radically different from their own. The same is not always true of the Tiger, though in this matching the Tiger would at least take the lead most of the time.

TIGER MEETS DRAGON

Here we have two creatures who are famous for their claws, even if in the case of the Tiger these weapons of war tend to be retracted for most of the time. It's true that the Dragon person would find the average Tiger type to be very attractive, and the same may also be true in reverse, for a while at least. A major problem comes because it is the natural lot of the Dragon to be in charge, both of people and of situations. This would not suit the average Tiger at all, who sees his or her ability to come and go at will as being fundamental. Sooner or later the sparks will begin to fly here!

TIGER MEETS SNAKE

The Tiger is basically an easy-going person, as long as things are going the way that it wants them to. Fortunately the Snake is very similar in this regard, despite the fact that the basic natures of these individuals are radically different. Each is also capable of being flexible, though probably not with each other. It's all a matter of principles. When your partner accepts that your point of view is valid and sound, you can afford to let matters ride, even allowing the other party to have their own way most of the time. It's only if there have to be significant arguments when it comes to putting your point of view across that you begin to think that you do really have a monopoly on the truth. Unless care is taken, life for the Tiger and the Snake could be like this all the time.

TIGER MEETS HORSE

In classic Chinese astrology, this association is seen as being particularly favourable. The Tiger, although quieter than the Horse, inclines towards the same positive outlook on life, and might even add a little extra spice to the Horse's usual exciting life. Times of confrontation would be few and far between, with the Horse and the Tiger both approaching situations from essentially the same direction. Social life would be active and the combination of two such cheerful characters brings a sunny and warm outlook and a degree of happiness that should extend to the wider family. Although the home would be important to both these types, they would be more likely to be found out and about in the community for most of the time.

TIGER MEETS GOAT

The Goat tends to be a fairly retiring creature and since although the Tiger is easy to like and can appear to be quite gregarious, it is underneath a fairly retiring creature too. Always the Tiger works best when pitted against another outgoing sign and so this might prove to be a fairly quiet match. However, the Goat is a good home-maker, likes to entertain and so would put out the welcoming mat for the original and even strange acquaintances that a Tiger person would bring around. There are two alternative forms of love here, since the Goat is emotional and the Tiger cerebral.

TIGER MEETS MONKEY

Here we have what amounts to two opposites, though the law of physics being what they are, it should be remembered that even opposites can attract. The Tiger finds it somewhat difficult to understand the capricious and occasionally lordly ways of the Monkey who often has a basically materialistic outlook on life which contradicts that enjoyed by the Tiger. However, Monkeys are singularly attractive people and Tigers do love beauty no matter what form it comes in. Because of this, we may be looking at an initial attraction, coming more from the direction of the Tiger which is likely to work well, only by significant effort on both sides. In its better moments, the Monkey can bring the Tiger more into the mainstream of life.

TIGER MEETS ROOSTER

Any problem here may manifest itself through communication, for although the Rooster can be something of a gossip, this person is not the most talkative individual in the menagerie. All the same, one thing that the Rooster can be good at is nagging and since Tiger people are rarely where they should be at the right time, this could prove to be a thorn in the side of the over-fastidious Rooster. Meanwhile, little irritates the Tiger, but it cannot stand being told where to be and when. Since there is a degree of stubbornness, albeit of a different kind, coming from both directions this could be a recipe for an irresistible force meeting an irremovable object.

TIGER MEETS DOG

The Dog is a very happy character. Easy going, chatty and friendly. All factors that the equally affable Tiger would recognise and like. However, perfection may be impossible to find outside the gates of heaven, and we do discover in this relationship the tendency to prevaricate. Both Dogs and Tigers are inclined to let matters slide, so together they could live a fairly disjointed life. Not that this should turn out to be too much of a problem, since any mess they manage to create in common is equally likely to be resolved together.

TIGER MEETS PIG

Pig people are sensualists at heart, a fact that any Tiger individual would find a little difficult to come to terms with. In addition, Pigs are inclined to be insecure and there is little that a Tiger mate could do to improve this situation. How could they, when the average Tiger person doesn't know for him or her self what it is going to be doing in 10 minutes, let alone be in a position to inform its partner of the fact. This would certainly be a worry to the Pig individual and perhaps with the passing of time even an irritant. It may be possible for the emotional content of the Pig's nature to understand the more mental pursuits enjoyed by the Tiger, though even this could prove difficult. Happiness in this case would come with absolute trust on both sides and more flexibility from the Pig.

RABBIT MEETS RABBIT

Oh dear! This is a match made in heaven. Unfortunately we don't live in heaven. There is much sensitivity in this pairing, but it is doubtful that anything truly practical would ever get done. The level of mutual understanding would be high, but the Rabbit nature goes so deep that for both partners, life could be like swimming in a bottomless lake. Any observer would notice that the quality of love exhibited between two Rabbits is obvious through every facet of life, so that all in all this is potentially the most ideal of relationships or perhaps the most difficult. There would be a certain lack of personality and spontaneity.

RABBIT MEETS DRAGON

The Dragon can be a fearsome beast, and without even intending to do so could even intimidate the retiring and shy Rabbit. However, there is great understanding down there in the burrow and the typical Rabbit person finds something to love in almost any individual, even the dynamic Dragon. There is an inclination for the Dragon person to want to place a protective arm around its Rabbit mate and in some cases this makes for a life-long attachment of great intensity. From a practical standpoint, the Dragon obviously takes the lead.

RABBIT MEETS SNAKE

These individuals could turn out to be fairly happy, if only because the demands they make upon each others are so limited. This may not be the best recipe for dynamism or for practical success in life, but it should spell a peaceful home-life with plenty of relaxation and no little sensuality creeping in. Probably the best world that the Snake and the Rabbit could live in together would be one in which it was possible to move towards mutual objectives steadily, but with a little of the determination that both the signs lack on occasions. Outside influences would be very important and somewhere along the line, originality and physical action would have to be introduced. The Snake is naturally more inclined to take significant periods of rest than the Rabbit, though even here a good compromise should be possible.

RABBIT MEETS HORSE

Some success has been noted with this combination. The gregarious Horse forms an ideal opposite to the more sensitive and generally quiet Rabbit. Nevertheless, it should be remembered that Rabbit people, though generally reserved, can be persuaded to come out into the open and there is no one better to do it than the Horse person. Horses are usually generous and fairly encouraging, though they may be somewhat impatient if the Rabbit doesn't come up to scratch quickly enough. Looked at from the other side of the fence, the Rabbit could become anxious, particularly on those occasions when it's Horse mate still hasn't returned home at 3 a.m!

RABBIT MEETS GOAT

As an archetype, this relationship should be ideal. Both sides are emotional and are home-makers. There is a great capacity for love and understanding, though perhaps just a slight absence of originality. Things could become a little too comfortable and especially if material considerations are well catered for, we could see boredom creeping in at some stage. It is important for both the Rabbit and the Goat to express themselves as voluably as possible to the world at large and to stay out there in the mainstream of social events. There will be few conflicts of interest and the addition of a family would be equally pleasing to both parties.

RABBIT MEETS MONKEY

The Monkey is a magnanimous type and would not set out deliberately to tie the less powerful Rabbit into knots, but may be unable to avoid doing so. However, most Rabbit individuals are deeply intuitive and could come to understand what truly motivates the apparent pride and even on occasion arrogance of the Monkey. Once this is established, a deep understanding could follow, with love not far behind. The mundane practicalities of life have to be dealt with. In this case, probably more by the Rabbit, though the Monkey person is a hard worker and would contribute well to family finances, which should be reasonably good. There is significant luck with both these signs and good foresight.

RABBIT MEETS ROOSTER

For most of the time, these two animals inhabit entirely different areas of the farmyard, for although both are generally reserved by nature, the Rooster has a tendency to strut and can be very opinionated. Nothing would be more inclined to disturb the peaceful existence of the Rabbit, than to be constantly reminded of its shortcomings, and since the Rooster could hardly fail to recognise them, even if they only exist in its own mind, they would certainly be spoken about. Even Rabbit people will only stand so much, and so in the fullness of time there could be fireworks here. Materially speaking the relationship is a good one, and a careful nurturing of resources on both sides is likely.

RABBIT MEETS DOG

The prognosis here is really very good. The kindness which is so much a natural part of the Rabbit nature is reciprocated by the faithful and caring Dog. There could be an instant rapport which is likely to be built upon as the two get to know each other more deeply. Conversation would rarely be a problem, since the Dog is not the kind of person to suppress the sometimes weak tendencies of the Rabbit which in this case can announce its own opinions and ideas. Neither of these signs is particularly conventional, and so one could expect an original relationship with a preference for travel.

RABBIT MEETS PIG

There is a distinctive liking and a deep understanding here, which makes the prognosis for this relationship extremely good. Its particularly hard for some signs to come to terms with the Pig, who can on the one hand be opinionated and on the other deeply sensitive. Coping with this situation comes as second nature to the affable Rabbit and the emotional content of the relationship would be extremely high. Since both individuals look at life in a similar way, arguments ought to be few and far between, though it might be suggested that the Pig's understanding of the Rabbit is probably not quite so good, since Pig types are more inherently selfish in the first place. The basic motivation is towards family and the home.

DRAGON MEETS DRAGON

A formidable combination this one, for one Dragon in a relationship can be quite a handful, let alone two. Certainly there will be dynamism and great enterprise; and since like poles often repel, there could be one or two fireworks on occasions too. Versatility is the keyword, just as long as both parties are not constantly trying to upstage each other. Two Dragons in the same relationship usually spells a busy partnership, with both parties willing and able to contribute to the overall success that can generally be expected. Confidence is not in short supply and there is usually the smell of success when two Dragons meet.

DRAGON MEETS SNAKE

The Dragon and the Snake can form a pretty workable partnership, just as long as each knows the basic nature and the shortcomings of the other. Since the Dragon is all activity, whilst the Snake is not adverse to a rest in the sun now and again, there could be some slight conflict as to what should be next on the agenda at any particular point in time, though this can easily be overcome with just a little careful consideration on both sides. The Snake is a careful planner, and once it has thought long and hard about a particular project, who would be better to put it into operation than the more dynamic Dragon? Personal relationships could be a slightly different kettle of fish however, since both signs are inclined to be stubborn in their own particular ways.

DRAGON MEETS HORSE

There should be few real obstacles on the path to success here, especially since the Horse person is inclined to make allowances for others, and in any case is capable of charming the fruit down from the trees when necessary. This would be an active and vibrant relationship, with something going on all the time. The mixing would be on a mental as well as a personal level and the social implications for these two signs working together are really very good. Confidence exudes from both Dragon and Horse, though the Horse is sometimes less confident than it appears and the Dragon can help out here.

DRAGON MEETS GOAT

This match depends to a great extent on the nature of the Goat person involved in the relationship. Many Goats are happy to find a protective arm thrown around their shoulders, in which case there is every chance of success, since the Dragon is always willing to take the strain. The Dragon is also happy when he or she knows that there is someone to come home to, an individual who is solid and reliable and who may take more responsibility in the home than the Dragon is willing or able to do. Goats love to please and are not usually adverse to living with a more dominant type, just as long as they are not subjected to life with a bully, which they will not tolerate.

DRAGON MEETS MONKEY

Here we have two individuals with a great deal in common. Both are inclined to be a little fiery by nature, so the sparks are almost certain to fly on occasions, though the Monkey and the Dragon really do respect individuals who stand up for themselves and will easily forgive and forget whenever necessary. With a get-up-and-go attitude to life on both sides there would be rarely a dull moment in this household. Material success should be a possibility, though both signs are inclined to take too many chances and so life could be just a little precarious on occasions.

DRAGON MEETS ROOSTER

There are occasions when the Dragon is inclined to fly too high for its own good, no matter how dynamic it is inclined to be. If drive and enthusiasm, careful planning and a steady approach to life are worth considering as a good basis for a relationship, then here we see an ideal match. The Rooster is a careful sort of person, though not one adverse to either success or material gains. In the planning stages of any operation, a Rooster is good to have around, and this wily old bird is also capable of working long and hard to achieve its objectives. The Dragon really does respect this attitude to life, even if it looks out at the world in a very different way itself. Peace should be possible in this household, just as long as the Rooster manages to put the brakes on its occasional nagging.

DRAGON MEETS DOG

The Dog is probably the most flexible character in the Chinese Animal Zoo, and yet here we have a match that is probably very unlikely to work well. Why? Well for a start because these signs are astrological opposites, though this is really fudging the issue. The real problem may well be that the Dragon really 'cares' about being successful in life, whilst the easy-going Dog looks at the whole business in an entirely different way. It is also true to say that in a relationship the Dragon needs someone to rely on, which may not work out all that well if the Dog is the individual in question. Dog people often think irrationally, and this can really annoy a Dragon.

DRAGON MEETS PIG

Although at first sight it may appear that this is a meeting of opposites, particularly as far as basic nature is concerned, it is not out of the question that there could be a real understanding forged in this relationship, given a little time and much understanding on both sides. Even in the case of the sensitive Pig there is great power underneath, a fact that the Dragon is likely to understand on an instinctive level. The Dragon may also come to realise that you can only push a Pig-type so hard. In return the Pig will offer great loyalty and might make a comfortable alternative to the Dragon's busy professional schedule.

SNAKE MEETS SNAKE

It might seem at first that there is very little happening inside this relationship. After all the Snake is a very low-key type, not boastful, though perhaps a little vain, and two Snakes in the same household are very unlikely to upset the neighbours. All the same there is a great capacity for slow and steady work and an ability to talk things through in a reasonable manner. Confusion could be kept to a minimum and that means that an ordered life is possible, which both Snake A and Snake B will very much appreciate. When it comes to free time or holidays, you will find this pair in the garden or on the beach, as Snakes love to be out in the fresh air. A good match this, though very heavy on sun-screener.

SNAKE MEETS HORSE

Nothing is impossible in life and so it is just likely that these characters will find a way to live happily together, though astologically the chips are stacked against them. The main problem lies in the very different approach to life that is adopted. The Snake likes to stay at home, finds it impossibe to rush anything and takes a rather slow and reptilian approach to life, whereas the Horse person is just the opposite in almost every respect. The natural tendency for certain types to come together in the first place may preclude this meeting on a romantic level. If not, there is a good deal of work necessary on both sides to bridge the innevitable gap.

SNAKE MEETS GOAT

An average association, that of the Goat and the Snake. Why? Probably because both these signs really do need the input that comes from a more dynamic character if they are to express themselves to the full. True, they can make a comfortable home and can work well together to build for the future. Chances are though that they will live fairly low-key lives and will not be the sort of couple to take risks of any sort. On a personal level there will be a good deal of love. but perhaps very little in the way of adventure.

SNAKE MEETS MONKEY

It could seem that the Snake person, for all his or her natural charm and affability is not the easiest person to match up with other Chinese signs. Certainly this may not be the best relationship potentially. Monkey types are go-getters and need to feel that there is always something around that they can get their teeth into. They love a challenge and will happily take a risk if the odds look even reasonably good. The same could not be said for people born under the sign of the Snake. Here we have a slower and more thoughtful approach to life. Money tends to be earned on a year in and year out basis, piled carefully away and spent wisely. Both signs do like to have a good time socially and it is possible that this could be the saving grace of the relationship. The Monkey is also just as loyal as the Snake, which in itself is a strong point.

SNAKE MEETS ROOSTER

The potential for success shines out from this pairing. The Rooster and the Snake come together from a common acceptance of the necessities of life and how best to get them. Both these signs have an earthy honesty and an understanding of the way things really are, and this could be the hallmark of a happy union. Security is most important here, and unlike some other signs, the Rooster can feel confident that a Snake spouse will help to bring home the bacon. The Snake and the Rooster would have similar ideas about recreation, holidays and general interests. They would also have the same standards concerning the raising of a family.

SNAKE MEETS DOG

It would be hard for almost any sign to find fault with the diplomatic and easy-going Dog, and the Snake is quite happy to fall under the hypnotic spell as a rule. Some of the Dog person's attitudes to life could be rather a bind to the Snake type, who prefers to know exactly what is going on, where and why. This is not really the case for the Dog, who tends to make up the story as he or she goes along. There is enough general understanding between these two for such considerations to be put on one side, though aspects of them could emerge in argument. The Snake is definitely the power behind any Doggy throne!

SNAKE MEETS PIG

One is left, in this case, with the feeling that there would be a distinct lack of useful communication between the Snake and the Pig, which could set the two off on a bad footing. Some authorities consider this to be a difficult and lack-lustre sort of match and it is true that neither the Snake or the Pig work at their best in isolation, which may prove to be the case if both these people run true to their sign. Strangely enough, when in the right sort of company, both the Snake and the Pig can be quite chatty, though probably not with each other. It must be remembered that these signs are opposites astrologically speaking and so their view on life, although to the outsider appearing to be very similar, is, in reality, very different.

HORSE MEETS HORSE

This is an interesting and reactive pairing. As with all associations of the same sign, two Horse types would have much in common. However, this would not always lead to a harmonious situation since Horse individuals need to be the centre of attraction and might find themselves overshadowed on occasions. Both parties have a love of life and a need to make things happen and to this extent can often be found together out in the world at large making life fun for themselves and everyone around them. The personal side of this relationship may prove to be problematic since Horses are not the most steadfast lovers.

HORSE MEETS GOAT

It is not uncommon to find Horse individuals being attracted to and often living with those people who were born under the sign of the Goat. There are good compromises on both sides here and the essential differences in nature tend to compliment each other. Although the Horse is gregarious, outgoing, conversational and fairly unpredictable, the steadfast and steady Goat compensates by remaining quiet and remaining willing on many occasions to take a back seat. However, this would not always be the case since even the Goat can be opinionated on occasions and would only let the Horse type go so far.

HORSE MEETS MONKEY

Not generally considered to be a wonderful match this. The basic problem would appear to be that both Horse and Monkey in their own respective ways want to be the centre of attraction. In the case of the Monkey, this means being in charge, but simply try to catch a wild mustang and train it and you will understand why Horse people are difficult to pin down. This would certainly lead to frustration with regard to the Monkey who is also a fixed type and expects situations to remain intrinsically the same from one day to the next. If a deep understanding could be established, then both happiness and success might follow. However, ultimate problems may be the Monkey's rather than those of the Horse and it is from the direction of the Money that arguments could come.

HORSE MEETS ROOSTER

In an astrological sense, there is some understanding here since according to Western practitioners at least, both these signs are ruled by the same planet. However, they tend to use this rulership in radically different ways and though both are basically communicators, it is the Horse's way to know a little about everything, whilst the Rooster definitely sets out from the word go to be an expert. Roosters are fairly pedantic and are even plodders on occasion. The symbolism remains valid here, for whoever heard of a chicken managing to keep pace with a stallion. However, the Rooster can show a strong inclination to guide the Horse whose very flexibility might make it possible for him or her to respond positively to this situation.

HORSE MEETS DOG

Full marks for this coming together, since both signs are of the same basic type. The Dog is of course an accommodating individual and is more likely to make allowances for the Horse's capricious and changeable nature than any other sign of the Chinese zodiac. Both signs are full of fun, so this is not a stay at home relationship, but one that involves the whole world outside the family door. Both Dog and Horse can be adventurous and in nature, as in people, both are capable of running long and hard without tiring too much.

HORSE MEETS PIG

There may be a slight lack of understanding here, probably more from the direction of the Pig, a steady and fairly fixed individual who could feel a little ill-at-ease with the gregarious nature and sometimes foolish antics of the Horse individual. Of course there are benefits; the Horse is in a good position to offer the less certain Pig a greater degree of confidence and there is certainly personal attraction with this combination since many Pig types would simply love to have the communication skills enjoyed by the Horse. Sexual magnetism exists within this pairing, but it is fair to suggest that the Pig may tire first probably desiring more continuity than the Horse is either willing or able to offer. It may be in the sphere of personal relationships that potential problems arise.

GOAT MEETS GOAT

Although a quiet affair this, there is no reason why two Goats should not live long and happily together. True they would not make much impression on the world at large, though on the other hand, they may not seek to do so. This union brings a slow and steady build-up towards mutually desired goals and an ability to plan carefully for the future. Neither participant would be full of character at the start and may not receive the confidence to develop one, which would be the case if they were attached to a more dynamic Chinese sign. However, there will be great mutual love and trust, little likelyhood of misunderstandings and possibly great contentment.

GOAT MEETS MONKEY

Although Goat people tend to be quiet, and are somewhat retiring by nature, this is not a sign that will be forced into doing anything and herein lies the potential difficulty when the Goat and the Monkey come together. Monkey people simply have to be in charge, they cannot help themselves and again without realising, they are inclined to stamp their authority particularly on those individuals they see as being less strong. It might appear that the Goat falls into this category, but this will almost certainly lead to trouble further down the line for all Goats have horns and can easily fight back if pushed.

GOAT MEETS ROOSTER

The average Goat individual, although compliant and generally understanding, does have a predilection for doing things in its own sweet way. This may not always suit the Rooster, who though also reserved is inclined to rule the roost in no uncertain terms. Moodiness and sulking could be the result if either individual felt that their own personal choices were being ignored. True there will be no steady stream of abuse, and peace may permeate this household, except for the occasional clucking of the Rooster. Attention to detail is important to both signs and so the home would be spotless and hygienic, if perhaps somewhat quiet. A good combination of signs for making money and for taking every opportunity of improving their common lot in life..

GOAT MEETS DOG

Very few individuals tend to fall out with the Dog, though the Goat is as likely to find fault with this sign as any other. The main reason would appear to be the danger of personality clashes, for even the diplomatic skills of the Dog cannot entirely cope with the depth of silence which the Goat is capable of. At heart, Goat individuals are loners and want to wander around, free to do what takes their fancy, even if many of these flights tend to be of a purely mental nature. For all its procrastination, the Dog is a doer and may sometimes find that the Goat is tardy in keeping up. However, such is the understanding of both sides that no problem in this case is insurmountable.

GOAT MEETS PIG

Here we find the basis for a harmonious coming together. Emotions are strong in the case of both these animal types, with the Pig possibly predominating in terms of latent aggression and a positive approach to life. This is not to infer that the Goat would be a follower. These animal types can walk hand in hand through life bringing great happiness to themselves in all they encounter. Neither would allow the world to be critical of the other and there would be genuine concern for the world at large coming from the direction of this relationship.

MONKEY MEETS MONKEY

Monkey people together tend to bring out the sunshine of the sign most noticeably and although there may be the occasional strained atmosphere, there can also be great happiness exuding from this pairing.

Underlying the basic relationship will be a constant struggle to see who will be in charge, with the pendulum swinging in one direction and then the other. As long as this fact is understood all should be well. This is a formidable working team and a pair who revel in wide open spaces, travel, change and diversity. Intellectual stimulus is important as is the ability to progress and to build on a happy atmosphere that both want to hold in common. Most important of all. the sense of purpose is the same in most situations.

MONKEY MEETS ROOSTER

It is hard to believe that the Monkey and the Rooster could have masses in common, though this relationship has often been tried with singular success. It would be important to the Monkey individual that the Rooster kept its farmyard strutting to other aspects of life and not as a means of criticising the relationship. Monkeys are freer by nature, more inclined to wander and indulge in a form of chatter that Rooster people would sometimes find a little irrelevant. The natural cheerfulness of the Monkey is however of great use in convincing the Rooster not to take life quite so seriously as it might otherwise do.

MONKEY MEETS DOG

The success or failure of this particular relationship is probably determined by the attitude and opinions of the Dog rather than of the Monkey. Since Monkey people tend to be rather forthright, and are quite happy to put their points of view in no uncertain terms, it requires the diplomacy of the Dog to balance situations. Both signs tend to take a fairly cheerful approach to life and there should certainly be compromise over domestic details and family arrangements. Dog people are wanderers by nature, but probably do not show the same degree of constancy to relationships that would be the case with the Monkey.

MONKEY MEETS PIG

These individuals are inclined to bring out the amorous qualities within the Monkey and also act as a strong focus for the energy, enterprise and enthusiasm of which the Monkey is capable. However, such intensity does the Pig bring to life that even the Monkey with its wide experience may get bogged down in a kind of emotional miras which runs very contrary to its own nature. Personality clashes are possible, out of which the Pig will be responsible for silences that the Monkey will find difficult, or perhaps even impossible to break. It is to this aspect of sorting out problems that most energy on both sides must be given, for the Monkey is a communicator at heart, whereas the Pig is not.

ROOSTER MEETS ROOSTER

The outside observer of this relationship would almost certainly be left with the impression that the household established by two Roosters was not only the most tidy and well-ordered place but probably also the most pedantic.. It's true that since at heart Rooster types consider themselves to be really quite 'together' types, they are likely to have the same view of a fellow member of the chicken run and in a way this might bring some poetic justice. Why? Because only by living with another of its own kind for any length of time will the average Rooster know what it can be like to be on the receiving end of such a careful and over-attentive sign.

ROOSTER MEETS DOG

Not a wonderful match this on first impression and reasons are fairly obvious. Although a generally neat sort of person in general, the Dog is not really too concerned with appearances, which is certainly not the case with the Rooster. The Dog always wants to come and go as it pleases, whilst the Rooster has to be tied to a fairly inflexible routine in order to feel really comfortable. Whilst the Rooster glories in having a sense of purpose, Dog people are inclined to rest on an attitude that says 'Sufficient unto the day'. If success is possible here it only comes with a deep understanding and real charity.

ROOSTER MEETS PIG

For all their strong points and in spite of the genuine good that most Rooster people bring to the world, it has to be said that this sort of individual is something of 'an acquired taste' and is rather unlikely to be on the Pig's menu. The Pig is a sesual type, which ought to mean that the two signs have much in common. However, Rooster desires are rather clinical and have a sort of ruthless logic about them which is very difficult to fault. The Pig is a passionate type whose desires spring from a much deeper well, yet one that it does not have either the knowledge or the words to explain. At worst, Roosters live on logic, whilst the Pig is out there considering only the emotion in situations. If there is a meeting point, it only really comes with time and a significant stretching of credibilities.

DOG MEETS DOG

This relationship has got to stand a better than average chance, if only because Dog types understand themselves and others all too well. This is a sign that can realise its own weaknesses all too readily, so there is no wonder that it can look at another Dog person with a certain amount of compassion, not to mention a basic knowledge of how to keep on the right side of him or her. Dogs are easy-going sorts in any case and can live in relative harmony with many other types of individuals, so in this case there ought to be even more in the way of love, trust and deep understanding. After all it's hard to fall out with your own reflection!

DOG MEETS PIG

The Dog and the Pig could easily make a go of life together. If they manage to cross the first hurdle and are attracted to each other, then here we find the basis for a good understanding. The Pig can see the roguish qualities of a Dog person, without taking them too much to heart. Meanwhile the Dog is more than able to supply the emotional fodder that is more important to any Pig than is real food. Both signs are family minded and could gradually cultivate a mutual understanding on a wealth of other matters too. Arguments should be few and far between.

PIG MEETS PIG

The sign of the pig is strange in some ways, for though it can live happily and at ease with a number of signs, there are some combinations that for one reason or another, just do not seem to work very well. The Pig and Pig scenario may be one such example. Part of the problem is that Pigs have to be with people who have the ability to make them talk, to express their deepest emotions. This prevents internalising situations that are almost certain to cause problems further down the line. Two Pig types living together may never really get round to expressing their true feelings about anything. As a result there could be the odd minor explosion when both Pigs reach boiling point at the same time. However, the situation may be entirely different if only one of the individuals is a talker!

THE CHINESE MOON

The ancient Chinese believed that the duration of one Moon, that is from the New Moon on to the next New Moon, was ruled by one of the twelve animal signs. These correspond almost exactly with what advocates of Western Astrology have come to know as their 'Sun Sign'. Arguably, of all single factors in the astrological make-up of an individual, this is probably the most important. However, it should be remembered that in all forms of Astrology, it is the overall part played by all aspects that determines the nature. Work out from the table below what your Chinese Moon sign is and then read the relevant entry in the section that follows. You can also refer to the more complete descriptions of the Chinese signs at the front of the book. Together with your Animal Year sign, Element and Ascendant sign, the Chinese Moon sets the seal on your nature and indicates the sort of individual you truly are.

CHINESE MOONS AND WESTERN SUN-SIGN COUNTERPARTS

CHINESE MOON	WESTERN SUN-SIGN	OPERATIVE DATES
DRAGON	ARIES	Mar 21st - Apr 20th
SNAKE	TAURUS	Apr 21st - May 21st
HORSE	GEMINI	May 22nd - Jun 21st
GOAT	CANCER	Jun 22nd - Jul 22nd
MONKEY	LEO	Jul 23rd - Aug 23rd
ROOSTER	VIRGO	Aug 24th - Sep 23rd
DOG	LIBRA	Sep 24th - Oct 23rd
PIG	SCORPIO	Oct 24th - Nov 22nd
RAT	SAGITTARIUS	Nov 23rd - Dec 21st
OX	CAPRICORN	Dec 22nd - Jan 20th
TIGER	AQUARIUS	Jan 21st - Feb 19th
RABBIT	PISCES	Feb 20th - Mar 20th

RAT MOON

Rat Moon individuals have a great deal of energy and tend to be very enterprising. Willing to have a go at almost anything, Rats are generally cheerful and can be relied upon to throw themselves with abandon into any project that takes their fancy, though deal less well with jobs or situations that they find to be tedious or inconsequential.

It's hard to pull the wool over the eyes of the average Rat, who is a sociable creature but certainly nobody's fool. This type is not beyond a gamble, either in a financial sense or with regard to life itself. Despite the naturally gregarious approach to life the Rat is capable of exhibiting great self control, which is one of the reasons for the success that Rat people often enjoy in business, especially in a self-employed capacity. Rat people are charming in company, love to be at parties and other gatherings and are very good travellers. Rats are opportunists and can make the most of changing circumstances. Occasionally Rat types are accused of being shallow, but nearly all the breed love the cut and thrust of everyday life in the fast lane.

OX MOON

One of the steadiest of the Chinese signs, Ox Moon people are still capable of much real success in life, usually by dint of hard work and a capacity to concentrate well on the job in hand. There may not be as much flexibility here as some of those doing business with this type might wish, and that means there are occasions when the Ox person is difficult to deal with. This is certainly the case when it comes to persuading an Ox to do something that goes against the grain, which most impartial but truthful observers would tell you is impossible.

With a very practical approach to life the average Ox knows exactly where he or she is going and is quite willing to work towards an objective carefully, taking time out on the way to smell the flowers but not allowing any real stumbling block to get in the way. At least with the Ox it is fair to say that 'what you see is what you get' and you will not be misled by this type, since most members of this family tend to be truthful. There is latent aggression here, though only if the Ox is pushed to extremes and has no other way to deal with a situation.

TIGER MOON

Tiger Moon people are not the easiest types to understand, for although this is basically a gregarious sign, and one that revels in fun and games, Tigers can also be quiet and reserved on occasions. This is a rash breed, inclined to go to extremes and always on the lookout for adventure. Tigers hate to be tied down by convention and delight in being able to choose the next move in their lives, no matter how strange their behaviour might appear to outsiders. Indeed strangeness is part of the appeal of this sign, which has originality written all the way through it.

Paradox after paradox attends this individual, for although you are likely to find Tiger types traversing mountain passes and striving to cross the Atlantic single-handed, you may just bump into one at the next party you attend. When the Tiger is in company it generally longs to be alone, and when in isolation desires nothing more than the cut and thrust of polite conversation. Tiger people can be very creative and are often especially musical.

RABBIT MOON

What an affable type is the Rabbit. Refinement is obvious in almost all members of this clan, though sometimes of an aloof nature which can make the more intelligent Rabbits slightly remote and difficult to approach. This may not be so surprising in the case of such a generally friendly soul when it is understood that the Rabbit is, in any case, an isolationist at heart. Here we have a person who needs long periods of reflection and the chance to live a relatively carefree life if he or she is to give of their best to the world at large, and the best can be extraordinary to say the least. Rabbits revel in serving mankind, are selfless and kind, and will work long and hard for a worthy cause.

Often Rabbit people appear to be uncluttered in their approach to life, which in reality is far from the truth, for few could plumb the depths of the Rabbit's deep thought processes. Relationships can be something of a problem because the Rabbit is a romantic at heart and finds it difficult to believe that anyone would let it down. This proclivity for believing that others will 'come good' is never lost to the Rabbit.

DRAGON MOON

Dragon individuals probably comprise the most dynamic group in the whole of the Chinese zoo. They are go-getters, always on the lookout for an opportunity to improve their lot and willing to do almost anything to get where they most want to be in life. Dragons are dominant by nature and do not take kindly to interference of any sort. Sometimes accused of being rash and impulsive, most Dragons are, nevertheless, quite ethical in their approach and prefer to achieve their objectives by fair means.

There is great honesty in the Dragon nature, probably too much on occasions for this individual can be so blunt that he or she might spend a significant period each week apologising for what was said last week. Dragons can cope very well with adversity and soon bounce back from situations that would have other signs laid low for days or weeks. The most positive approach to life is reserved for work, at which the Dragon excels. Sales, administration and management all appeal to this larger-than-life individual.

SNAKE MOON

This is probably the most laid-back character of the bunch. The Snake is an affable person and loves to be loved. Although not especially go-getting and inclined on occasions to be somewhat lazy, the Snake is a surprisingly good worker once the call comes, and is very good at carving out a niche for itself in life. Snakes of both sexes are very clean types and are often to be found in the bath. They are inclined to put on a little weight unless care is exercised regarding the diet. for the average Snake is also very fond of food.

Being followers of fashion, it's a fair bet that Snakes will always look at their best under any given circumstance and since they are very socially inclined, you would often find them at parties and other gatherings that offer the chance to sparkle. Most Snakes have a very strong sex drive, and especially so the males of the species. They are attractive to the opposite sex, not only other Snakes but a wide variety of signs and types. The best place of all to locate the Snake person however is out in the sunshine. They love the open air and would hate to waste a warm, summer's day in the house.

HORSE MOON

We arrive at one of the most fun-loving types to be found anywhere. This character is always on the go. loves to be the centre of attraction and does everything possible to keep itself and everyone it comes across just as happy as possible. For all his or her high activity, the Horse is capable and can sort out almost any sort of mess in an instant. True this is not the most constant person you could expect to meet in a month of Sundays, which may be one of the reasons that relationship problems are more common here. Not that this is too much of a problem for the Horse person it is so easy to forgive almost any transgression.

One of the greatest gifts that most Horse types display is that of being able to persuade almost anyone to do anything. Which is why the Horse usually manages to get things going its own way. Comfort and security tend to be of secondary importance and the Horse is a great lover of freedom in all its various forms. Despite a tendency to pretend the contrary is true, the Horse type is not easily fooled.

GOAT MOON

It may be an obvious insecurity that singles the Goat out as being a fairly retiring person on first impression, plus the fact that this character is never going to be the loudest at any gathering, not even when it really does understand what is expected of it. The Goat loves to please, but will not shake off its non-materialistic qualities, nor will it miss any opportunity to show what a cultured person should really be like. Visit any opera or art gallery and you will be able to number a significant collection of Goat people amongst the patrons.

The Goat tends to be a fairly lucky person and though not really willing to take too many chances with money, which it is careful to look after, it seems to attract more than its fair share all the same. Not that the average Goat is interested in cash for its own sake. Most Goats are family types and love to keep a good home where even outsiders would be made to feel welcome. The Goat is a demure and yet very uninhibited lover and wants to do all that it can to create and maintain a happy marriage. All Goat people look for security.

MONKEY MOON

Here we find a most versatile individual, one who is always on the go and who gets a great deal of pleasure out of life. Monkey people like to be in the news, at the centre of almost any activity and will be happy to help out whenever they can. Monkeys are fashionable and are capable of looking good at almost any time. They will set out to have a good time at the drop of a hat and are almost always to be found in the company of equally likeable and gregarious types.

In a relationship sense the Monkey can be a very provocative type of person, though this should not infer any tendency towards immoral behaviour, even though the Monkey can also be a plotter and is known to be quite deceptive on occasions. Gifted with a good memory, the Monkey is more like an elephant in that it rarely forgets anything and will always trade a good turn for one of its own sooner or later. This cheeky type has a large ego and really does like to mix with people who are both attractive and interesting. Monkeys love to be going 'somewhere' in life.

ROOSTER MOON

There may not be a more practical type than the Rooster, which is why so many people born under this sign seem able to turn their hands to almost anything. If you had to be cast up on a desert isle the Rooster would be an ideal person to have around, though not in every respect. True the Rooster could lay on a water supply and might be good at builing a place to live. Your Rooster Friday would be attentive and chatty, and would always be willing to talk things over at the end of a long day. On the other hand they would also probably nag you if things were not going the way they wished and might even make your life difficult if you were not the sort of person who could cope with this singular type.

The Rooster individual does not set out to upset anyone, and indeed would probably shrug his or her shoulders at the prospect. All the same, in adition to being one of the kindest and most capable people you would ever want to meet, the Rooster is almost certainly one of the most infuriating too. You can at least rely on consistency here, together with a good ability to make and hang on to money.

DOG MOON

The Chinese Dog person turns out to be almost everyone's cup of tea, and why not? This individual is charming, diplomatic and understanding. Although sometimes just a little too outspoken for its own good, the Dog type is also willing to listen to what you have to say, and this may be one of the reasons why the Dog is so hard to dislike. Dog people can be far too anxious on occasions and will often worry about the sort of details most people would barely give a thought to. This is mostly because the Dog finds it more or less impossible to make up its mind about anything and so consequently is always on the verge of changing horses in mid-stream. This quality is sometimes rather unfortunate and does condition the Dog into expecting the worst of situations. Having made up its mind regarding this eventuality, it comes as no surprise to the Dog when things actually do manage to go wrong, almost a self-perpetuating prophecy. Dog types love to have other people around, are very understanding and make the finest and most considerate of lovers.

PIG MOON

Even though the Pig Moon person is not the most outspoken of the Chinese signs, you could never fail to know when there is one around. The Pig is kind and usually understanding and is especially good to those it takes to, which includes family members to whom it is especially attached. Pigs are astute and can easily attract and hoard money. They are good workers, are keen to get ahead and always find their way to the front of the queue in one way or another. Although a little coy when first approaching a new relationship, this is no reflection on the way that the Pig will turn out to be ultimately. This person is very broad minded and although generally true in relationships the Pig is a sensualist in every sense of the word, so that a good sexual relationship is certainly important.

The Pig person does much on behalf of the various charities that it chooses to support and is often to be found in one of the professions that is geared towards helping others in one way or another. Perhaps most important of all, despite being strong-willed, the Pig is also capable of being flexible.

Opening
doors to
the World
of books

BOOK TOKEN

Book
Tokens

Book Tokens
can be
bought and
exchanged
at most
bookshops